Lent and [ ]
Reflections [ ]
the Younger
Crowd

JOHN BEHNKE, CSP

Paulist Press
New York/Mahwah, NJ

Cover and book design by Lynn Else

Copyright © 2010 by Paulist Press, Inc.

ISBN: 973-0-8091-4633-8

Library of Congress Control Number: 2009938882

Published by Paulist Press
997 Macarthur Boulevard
Mahwah, New Jersey 07430

www.paulistpress.com

Printed and bound in the
United States of America

CONTENTS

Contents

INTRODUCTION AND SUGGESTIONS FOR USING THIS GUIDE

This book of meditations is meant for the young person who, for many reasons—such as just having made a public profession of faith at a confirmation ceremony or having recognized a large growth step in becoming an adult—is ready to start on a journey of daily reflective prayer. Also, it would be of value to anyone who is, or would like to be, "young at heart."

Each meditation has four parts:

1. *Quick retellings of the Sunday, special day,*
   or weekday Scripture readings
2. *Further Reflection*
3. *Prayer*
4. *My Thoughts*

The approach emphasizes the use of ordinary language and everyday experience to assist the user of this guide to develop a pattern of prayer, reflection, and daily meditation.

The readings are in and of themselves "Scripture-based meditations" and not necessarily even paraphrases. These have been especially designed in a way to help supplement, ***not substitute*** for, the actual reading of the scriptural texts that are assigned to be used for the Lectionary on a given day. The author has reflected on the passages of selected Scripture verses and consulted the commentaries. The verses have been restructured in more modern and familiar speech patterns that would be somewhat more appealing to the young-at-heart mind, capturing, hopefully, the gist of the text, although not becoming immersed in a precise scholarly rendition of the ancient texts themselves. The author's intent is an easy-to-read primer to help initiate the almost adult person into the joys and peace of spirit and mind one gains through personal contact with God that can be achieved by means of a structured meditation.

The daily "readings" and *reflections* are meant as an aid to the young, meditative neophyte. They are considered as grist material and as a jumping-off point to be followed up with a quiet period of time in conversation and prayer with God.

The unfinished *prayer* at the end of each meditation is a further aid in achieving, hopefully, quality prayer-time. The users of this meditation book are encouraged to complete these unfinished prayers in their own words, searching the depths of their hearts for the prayers they would like express to the loving God we worship.

My thoughts was a later addition to this set of meditations when the possibility of publishing this resource was discussed. At the time, I was working in Minnesota at the Newman Center, where many students from the University of Minnesota attended services. We decided to have a specially selected group give their own reflection on my reflections. What started out to be a Lenten project ended up taking a whole year to complete.

I am especially grateful to this group of young men and women for their willingness to participate in this endeavor and extremely grateful that they were willing to give permission to be a part of this publication and to have their names appear in print. Their personal thoughts have added tremendously to the impact this set of meditations will have on those who use it in their prayer life.

May this resource help your spiritual journey to meditate upon the Scriptures, find new ways to pray, and live as a Christian follower of Jesus.

PART I
SUNDAYS AND SPECIAL DAYS

ONE
SUNDAYS OF LENT

First Sunday of Lent (Cycle A)

Genesis 2:1–9, 3:1–7

After finishing creating the world, God made the first man and woman. God called one Adam and the other Eve. God gave them a beautiful place called Eden to live in. They had everything they needed to live and be happy. They had plenty of food to eat. They had lots of places to visit. They had many different things they could do. One day, however, the devil came to Eve and said, "Why do you think God told you not to eat the fruit of that one special tree over there? Here, I'll pick one for you. They're really very delicious. Try one."

Eve didn't want to eat the fruit because she remembered that God had told her not to. After all, God had been really good to her and Adam. God gave them everything they ever needed. They were happy. She didn't need to taste the fruit of that one tree.

The devil kept trying to talk Eve into eating the fruit. It did look good. Her mouth was watering. Finally she gave in and took the fruit from the devil and ate it. Adam came by then and Eve talked him into taking a bite from it too. After they ate it, however, it didn't taste as good as they thought it would, because they knew that they had done something very bad. They had committed a sin. They had done the one thing God had told them not to do.

Psalm 51:3–6, 12–14, 17 *God, forgive us for the wrongs we've done*

God, forgive me. You are so good to me. I have done so many wrong things. Please give me the strength I need so that I will not sin anymore. Give me back true happiness. Help me always to do good.

Romans 5:12–19

St. Paul wrote a letter that said, We should thank God every day for giving us Jesus Christ. It was Jesus who showed us how to live really good lives. It was Jesus who saved us. If you remember, it was the first human on earth who brought sin into the world. His name was Adam. It was Jesus who saved us from our sins. Adam disobeyed God. It was Jesus who showed us how to love God fully.

Matthew 4:1–11

When Jesus returned from a trip, he decided that he needed to do some serious thinking by himself. So he spent about forty days praying and thinking and doing penance. While he was doing this, the devil tried to make Jesus do things that were not right.

The devil said to him, "If you really are the Son of God, take this stone I have in my hand and change it into bread." Jesus was very hungry because he had been spending most of his time praying and thinking, but he said to the devil, "God gave me special powers to help other people. God does not want me to use my special talents only to help myself." The devil didn't give up. He tried to tempt Jesus two more times, but Jesus never gave in. The devil finally went away, but that wasn't the last time he tempted Jesus. He came back many times during Jesus' life and tried to get him to do wrong.

Further Reflection

Jesus didn't give in to temptation. That's something I could work on a lot in my life.

Prayer

Dear God, I want to do what is right. Please help me to…

My Thoughts: Steve Jaeger

These reflections tell the stories in a more real and personalized light. Rather than just reading that the Bible says that such-and-such occurred, these reflections give the reader more detail, as if it were being witnessed before his or her very eyes. It focuses more on how one would feel if he or she was actually there. It's more personal. Ultimately, it helps the reader relate more easily to the passages.

❦

First Sunday of Lent (Cycle B)

Genesis 9:8–15

Noah built his ark and put all the different animals in it. He spent forty days and forty nights in it waiting for the rain to stop. Finally the rain stopped. A few days later the ark drifted to dry land, and Noah and his family got off and started to build a place to live. One day soon after, God came to Noah and his family and said, "I want to make a covenant with you. It's a very special covenant because I want it to last forever. I promise you that never again will the whole world be destroyed by a flood, like the one that just ended. And to show you that I mean it, from time to time I am going to put a beautiful rainbow in the sky. Every time you see the rainbow, you will know that I am still keeping my promise."

Psalm 25:4–9 *God, your ways are true*

God, teach me the way you want me to live. Show me what is right. Don't forget you've always been fair and square with us in the past. Please don't forget to be good to us now. God, you really are good. It's you who shows sinners how to live good lives. It's you who helps people find peace and justice if they ask you in a nice way.

1 Peter 3:18–22

St. Peter wrote a letter that said, Do you have any idea why Christ died for us? He died so he could show us the way to God. He gave his life for us. Do you remember hearing stories of how bad the people were in Noah's time? God destroyed all the bad people and then made a covenant with Noah and his family since they were the only people who were good. Noah and his family were saved by sailing over the flooded earth in their ark. Today, we are saved from sin, sort of in the same way, by being baptized. God saved Noah and his family from drowning. He saves us by baptism so that we can be with him always.

Mark 1:12–15

Just before Jesus started out on his preaching career, the Spirit of God working deep inside him made Jesus decide that he had better take some time off and think and pray about what he was doing, so he would be sure he was making the right choice in his life. The Spirit of God took him away from his family and friends and away from all the things that were going on in the city.

Jesus went out into the desert to a place where he knew it would be quiet and nobody would bother him. He spent forty days praying and thinking. A couple of times he was tempted to forget all about preaching and just go on doing what he wanted to do. But he finally decided that God wanted him to preach. He moved back into the city and started his preaching career. In his first sermon he said, "The time has come. It's time to stop living bad lives. It's time to start doing what God wants you to do. It's time to start loving all people." It scared Jesus to get up and say these things because just the week before, his friend John the Baptist was arrested for saying the same things.

Further Reflection

Forty days seems like an awfully long time to be doing penance until I realize how much God has already done for me.

Prayer

Dear God, help me to get as much out of this Lent as I can. Help me to change. Please help me to…

My Thoughts: Steve Jaeger

Forty Days....That is a long time. However, we should recognize, especially in a time where things are done in milliseconds, that proper reflection on ourselves and what God has done for us in our lives calls for lots of time. A lot can happen in forty days, but a lot has happened since the dawn of time for both humanity and ourselves. I think that history is worthy of being reflected upon. God is definitely worthy of a fraction of our lives.

❧❧•❧❧

First Sunday of Lent (Cycle C)

Deuteronomy 26:4–10

Moses said, "After you have given the priest your offering and he has placed it before the altar say, 'We bless you, our great God, because you have been with us and saved us and led us into this promised land flowing with milk and honey.' Then bow down in adoration. After that, rejoice because of all God has done for you."

Psalm 91:1–2, 10–15 *Be with me, God, especially when I am in trouble*

God, you are my refuge and my strength. You even send your angels to protect me. If I stumble, they will pick me up. Even wild animals will not harm me. When I call upon God, my prayers are answered.

Romans 10:8–13

St. Paul wrote in a letter that said, Do you remember what it says in Scripture? It says that the word is near, on your lips, and in your heart. If you profess your belief in Jesus and believe in your heart that God brought him back from the dead, then you will be saved. It doesn't matter who you are; as long as you believe this, you'll be saved.

Luke 4:1–13

Jesus went out into the desert for forty days where he fasted. During that time he was tempted by the devil. The devil said, "If you really are the Son of God, turn this rock into bread." Jesus replied, "People don't live on bread alone." The devil had a few more temptations to use on Jesus. He took him up on a high point and showed Jesus all the kingdoms of the world. "I'll give you all these kingdoms if you fall down and worship me," the devil said. It was tempting, but Jesus said, "The only one we should bow down before is God." Then the devil took Jesus to one of the Temple towers and said, "If you are the Son of God, jump off this roof. God's angels will save you." Jesus said back. "We're not supposed to test God." Jesus stumped the devil, so the devil left to figure out better ways to trick Jesus into following him.

Further Reflection

All through history God has been there helping, loving, and supporting us. Lots of times I get too sure of myself and think I can do it all; I can do anything. If I was honest with myself, I would have to admit that were it not for God, I couldn't do even the simplest of things.

Prayer

Dear God, be with me and help me, especially when I get those sudden urges to stray from the path that leads to you. Please help me to...

My Thoughts: Regina Munnelly

Without you, Lord, I can do nothing, but if you are there, anything and everything is possible. I find myself praying this silently even in the simplest situations. I don't know what I would do if God were not with me. I couldn't imagine it. A couple of years ago I was hit by a car. I am still sometimes fearful when it comes to crossing the street. I just have to say that silent prayer. What I have found is that the fear itself does not go away just because I have prayed that prayer, but I feel this confidence and even though I'm scared, I find I can still cross the street, but only because God is with me. This may seem stupid, but to me crossing the streets was a big fear of mine for a long time. I have been learning that if you just "give it to God" it will be OK.

❧❧•❧❧

Second Sunday of Lent (Cycle A)

Genesis 12:1–4

One day God said to Abraham, "I want you to leave this place. I want you to become a pioneer. I think it would be a good idea for you to build a new town in a place far away from here. Years after you are dead and gone, this town will grow into a city, and that city will grow into a great country. Your name will be famous. People will be proud to say that you were one of their ancestors."

Abraham listened to what God was calling him to do. He thought about it for a long time and then agreed to become a pioneer. He packed up his belongings, and with all of his family he started out on the trip, which would take a long time. The amazing thing about all of this was that Abraham was a very old man when God asked him to do this difficult task.

Psalm 33:4–5, 18–20, 22 *God, we need your help*

God, you always tell the truth. You are the one we can always trust. You are kind and loving to all. We pray to you. We feel your kindness and your presence in our lives.

2 Timothy 1:8–10

St. Paul wrote a letter that said, You already know that God sent Jesus to save us and to show us how to live good lives. Now it is up to us, with God's help, to live those good lives. Now it is up to us to help and care for those around us. Now it is up to us to tell people the good news about Jesus Christ!

Matthew 17:1–9

One day, Jesus and three of his close friends went up a mountain to pray together. Jesus' friends—Peter, James and John—were very tired and they fell asleep, so Jesus prayed by himself. While he was praying, he had a vision and talked with two saints from the Bible stories. Their names were Moses and Elijah.

While Jesus was talking to these famous people, Peter woke up and saw what was going on. Peter heard a voice coming out of the sky, saying, "This is my Son; listen to him." After the vision went away, Peter said, "Jesus, this must be a very holy place because you were talking to the saints right here. Let's build a church on this spot so that people can come and pray here, too." But Jesus told Peter that it was not the right time to tell the world about what had happened, and so they decided not to build the church.

Further Reflection

Jesus prayed with his friends. It's part of being human to pray for one another, and to pray together. It's one of the ways we gain our strength to do the things we need to do.

Prayer

Dear God, without you I can do nothing. Help me this day to do your will. Please help me to…

My Thoughts: Joe Curry

Help me to see the needs of those around me and the ways that I can lend my knowledge and abilities. Help me to listen for the words unspoken, for through silence much can be said. Allow me to hear my mission so that I may serve my community to the best of my abilities.

❧❧•❧❧

Second Sunday of Lent (Cycle B)

Genesis 22:1–2, 9–13, 15–18

Once a long time ago, there was a very holy man whose name was Abraham. God had a special job that had to be done. He wanted someone to become the father of a great nation. God wanted to choose Abraham for the job, but first he had to make sure that Abraham would do everything he told him to do, no matter what happened. God came up with a plan, so he said to Abraham, "Abraham, I'm going to ask you to do something for me. It's going to be very difficult for you to do it, but this is what I want you to do. I want you to go up that mountain with your son Isaac. When you get to the top, I want you to sacrifice Isaac as an offering to me."

Abraham didn't want to do it, but he knew that if that's what God wanted, it was the way it had to be. So Abraham took his son for a walk up the mountain. When they got to the top they built a small altar. Then, although he didn't want to, Abraham put his son on the altar (as God had asked him to do). He was just about to drive a knife into Isaac's heart when a messenger from God appeared and said, "Wait! Don't do it! All God wanted to see was if you would do anything he told you to do. He's convinced that you would. You don't have to kill your son."

Both Abraham and Isaac were very happy and relieved about that. They offered God another kind of sacrifice and then the messenger said, "Abraham, God is very pleased with the things you are doing. As a reward he wants to make you the father of a great nation."

Psalm 116:10, 15–19 *God, you are my God*

I believed in God even when I was having a difficult time. I even said back then, "God, I am here to do what you want. You are the one who saved me." God, I make many sacrifices in my life for you and I always pray to you for help. I will let everyone know that you are my God.

Romans 8:31–34

St. Paul wrote a letter that said, I've been doing some serious thinking lately. I've decided that if God is on our side, it doesn't really matter who doesn't like us. I'm sure God will help us whenever we need him because, after all, God's already sent Jesus to show us how to live.

Mark 9:2–10

One day, Jesus and three of his close friends went up a mountain to pray together. While Jesus was praying, he had a vision and talked to two saints from the Bible stories. Their names were Moses and Elijah. While Jesus was talking to these famous people, Peter heard a voice coming out of the sky saying, "This is my Son: listen to him." After the vision went away, Peter said, "Jesus, this must be a very holy place because you were talking to the saints right here. Let's put up some holy buildings on this spot so that other people can come and pray here too." But Jesus told Peter that it was not the right time to tell the world about what had happened, and so they decided not to make a fuss over what had happened.

Further Reflection

Jesus wasn't into hype. Jesus wasn't into the flamboyant. Everything he did was for a good purpose. The disciples needed to see Jesus in his glory, but the whole world didn't.

Prayer

Dear God, sometimes I jump the gun and blow things all out of proportion. Help me to keep a good perspective on life. Please help me to...

My Thoughts: Jenny Tomes

It's so easy to get caught up in the hype. Yet the further we're consumed, the further away our relationship with God gets. I've often found myself searching for God in chaos—only to find myself lost in trivial concerns of success, perfection, and happiness. It ends in a cycle of empty reward and painful awareness that, once again, I've hit a dead end. Somehow, after my rollercoaster of mayhem, God pulls me back—through a shooting star, a smile, someone else. It's always been the simple things—given with the simplicity of a wink, and comforting me like the warmth of an embrace.

❧❧•❧❧

Second Sunday of Lent (Cycle C)

Genesis 15:5–12, 17–18

God said to Abraham, "Look up into the sky. Can you see all those stars? I am so pleased with you that your descendants will be as many as there are stars in the sky. I am the God who helped you since you left your homeland of Ur. You and your descendants shall live in this land that you see before you. I give it to you." To seal the pact, Abraham made a huge sacrifice of animals to God.

Psalm 27:1, 7–9, 13–14 *I will walk in God's presence*

God is my light and my salvation. I am not afraid. God, I will praise your name at all times. Be with me always. You are my helper.

Philippians 3:17—4:1

St. Paul wrote a letter that said, I beg you to imitate the way I live, because I live the way Christ instructed us to live. If you stand firm in the Lord you will be pleased with the results.

Luke 9:28–36

Jesus took Peter, James, and John off by themselves. They went up on top of a nearby mountain where Jesus had an out-of-the-ordinary type of experience. He had a glow all about him and he was really talking with two prophets who had been dead for years. The apostles saw Moses and Elijah meeting with Jesus. Then a voice came out of a nearby cloud and said, "This is my beloved Son. Listen to him." Then all of a sudden all the apostles saw was Jesus standing alone. The apostles didn't tell anyone about this, but kept it to themselves.

Further Reflection

Abraham followed God's way. Jesus did God's will. Paul followed what Jesus preached. Our faith and our beliefs call us to do the same. I know, when I am walking in God's way, I feel much better about the world and myself. I also know, when I don't, I really don't feel good about myself. It makes practical sense to do it God's way.

Prayer

Dear God, wanting to do it your way, and then actually doing it, are two completely different things. Thinking is simple. Doing is harder. Please help me to...

My Thoughts: Zach Czaia

In all these passages we see strong men who have entrusted their lives to God. Where the world saw folly in these men, the Lord saw wisdom, and so he made Abraham a father to us all, David a courageous king, Paul a spokesman for the truth, and the outspoken fisherman Simon Peter the shepherd of the Church on Earth. Let us take solace in being different from those around us if our difference means we are following Christ's path and not the world's. As the apostles Peter, James, and John did, let us treasure our gift of faith in the silence of our hearts.

❧❦•❧❦

Third Sunday of Lent (Cycle A)

Exodus 17:3–7

When the Israelites escaped from slavery and went into the desert, their troubles weren't over. While they were wandering in the desert, many of them were starving because they didn't have enough food to eat. Many of them were also dying of thirst because there was very little water to drink in the desert. Many of the people began to get angry at Moses for thinking up this plan to escape. If you listened to them around their campfires at night, you could hear them say things like, "Why did we ever leave Egypt? Why did we ever listen to Moses? All we're going to do out in this hot desert is die of starvation and thirst!"

Moses knew what the people were saying, so he prayed to God, "God, help me. I don't know what to do. If these people get any angrier, they'll kill me." God knew that Moses was in trouble. God said, "Tonight, call the people together. Have them meet over by that big rock. When you get them together, I'll make water flow out of the rock. There will be more than enough for all of them to drink."

That night Moses did what God told him to do. When everyone saw the water come out, they quickly drank the water because they were thirsty. You could hear them shouting and laughing and praising God. "Surely God is in our midst," they shouted and prayed.

Psalm 95:1–2, 6–9 *If today you hear God's voice in your heart, follow it*

Come, everyone, let's sing to God. Let's tell the world that God has saved us. Let's thank God from the bottom of our hearts. Let's sings songs of praise to God. Come, let's bow our heads down and pray to God. In fact, let's kneel before God, who made us. Don't grumble or argue like the people in the desert did when everything didn't go the way they expected it to.

Romans 5:1–2, 5–8

St. Paul wrote a letter that said, Since Jesus has saved us, we are now at peace with God. God has sent us the Holy Spirit The Spirit helps us to live good lives. The Spirit gives us the courage to do what is right. It's amazing to sit back and think that Jesus did all this for us. He even died for us! And still sometimes we commit sins by doing things that are bad.

John 4:5–42

One day while Jesus was walking, he became very tired. He sat down by a well to rest for a while. He was thirsty, too, because it was very hot out, but he didn't have anything to pull the water out of the well with. Finally, after a long wait, a woman came by to get water for her home. When Jesus saw her coming, he jumped up and asked, "Will you give me a drink of water, please?" (Back in those days there were a lot of class distinctions and normally no one would ask that woman for anything. So naturally that woman was surprised by Jesus' question.)

She said, "Sir, no one like you has ever asked me for anything." Jesus surprised her again by answering, "If you knew who I was, you would be asking me to give you living water so that you would never thirst again." She said, "You sound like you're pretty important. Who are you—a prophet?" Jesus then told her things about herself, which only she and God could have known, so she believed that Jesus was a very holy person. He then explained to her what he meant when he said he was the living water and talked to her about doing good for other people and loving all people.

When she went home, she led many people to believe in Jesus and live good lives.

Further Reflection

I will never be able to totally live up to the example Jesus set for me to live. I may be able to be like the woman at the well who, after she believed, brought other people to that belief.

Prayer

Dear God, help me to not only live my beliefs but also to be willing to share them with people I come in contact with on a daily basis. Please help me to…

My Thoughts: Tom Klein

Nobody will ever be like Jesus, so what the woman did was as close to living in his likeness as we can get. We must believe in Jesus and work to spread his word to our neighbors. This is all we have to give to God.

❧❧•❧❧

Third Sunday of Lent (Cycle B)

Exodus 20:1–17

One day God said to his people, "Here are some rules I want you to always follow:

1. Pray only to me because I'm the one who made you and saved you.
2. I don't want to hear any of you swearing.
3. I want one day out of the week to be a special day for you. Don't do too much work that day so you can relax and spend some special time praying to me.
4. I want you to listen to your parents (even when you grow up) because they have lived longer and know more about life than you.
5. Don't kill anyone for any reason.
6. Don't fool around with someone you're not married to.
7. Don't take anything that isn't yours.
8. Don't lie about anybody.
9. Don't always be wanting things that belong to other people.

All I'm really asking is that you "love me and keep my rules."

Psalm 19:8–11 *God's laws are good laws*

The rules that God gives us are best. You can always depend on God's word. It is full of wisdom even for those who don't know too much. God's laws are really pretty good. They make you happy just to follow them. God's laws tell it like it is. God's laws are good and fair. They're worth more to me than all the gold in the whole world. I want to keep God's rules more than anything else in the world.

1 Corinthians 1:22–25

St. Paul wrote a letter that said, You know some people go through life expecting everything to be proved to them by miracles from God. Some people try to find the way of life by reading what somebody once wrote in a book and following what the book says *precisely*, without ever asking questions. When we preach about Jesus to these kinds of people, they think we're crazy. Some of them think it's the weirdest story they ever heard. They just don't understand that Jesus is the Son of God and he showed us how to live good lives.

John 2:13–25

A couple of days before a big, holy celebration was to take place, Jesus went to Jerusalem to be there ahead of time. That afternoon he decided to go to the Temple, the house of God, to say some prayers. When he got there, he looked around outside at God's beautiful house and then went in. As he looked around inside, he couldn't believe his eyes. There were lots of people there. Some of them were selling things. Jesus got so mad at what he saw that he started screaming, "Get out of here! What do you people think you're doing, anyhow? This isn't just some sidewalk where you can do anything you want. This is the house of God." At that point he was so angry he started pushing their tables over and he didn't stop until they were all out of there.

As the people were running out, someone shouted to Jesus, "What gives you the right to do this to us? Prove to us that you have the right!" Jesus said something very unusual at that point. He said, "If you destroy this place, I will rebuild it in three days." The people didn't understand what he was talking about because the Temple originally took about fifty years to build. But they were in such a hurry to get out of there that they didn't stop to ask Jesus what he meant. (But now we know that Jesus was actually talking about his death and resurrection and not just talking about an old building.)

Further Reflection

God certainly works in wonderful ways. The Israelites were sent King Cyrus to build the Temple. We were sent Jesus to build the kingdom. God provides for all times and all places and all peoples.

Prayer

Dear God, thank you for being you. Thank you for being in our lives and in our history. Please help me to…

My Thoughts: Will French

What these readings are saying to me is that God is a loving and caring God who will provide for us what we truly need. God wants us to be happy in our daily lives and to love our fellow human beings in the same way he loves all of us. God also understands that everyone needs to find their own image of God. They can't just read about him in an old book; they need to see God in the little things that happen to them every day. When people start to see glimpses of God in everyday things, they begin to form their own image of God.

❧❧•❧❧

Third Sunday of Lent (Cycle C)

Exodus 3:1–8, 13–15

While Moses was tending the flock near the mountain of God (Mount Horeb), he saw an angel of God in a burning bush. The real weird thing was that although the bush was on fire, it wasn't actually burning up. When he went over to get a closer look, God said to him, "Take your sandals off, this is a holy place. I am the God of your ancestors. I know the pain and suffering that my people are having in Egypt. You're going to lead my people to freedom. Tell them I'm the ONE, and I'm going to do this for them."

Psalm 103:1–4, 6–8, 11 *God is kind and merciful*

Bless God. Bless God's holy name. Remember all the good God has done for us. God is kind and compassionate. No one is kinder.

1 Corinthians 10:1–6, 10–12

St. Paul wrote a letter that said, I want you to remember that our ancestors were led out of slavery by Moses. It wasn't an easy escape. There were a lot of trials they went through. Some of them died before they got to the Promised Land. We're going to have trials in our life too. In a sense, they are the hurdles that make our faith stronger.

Luke 13:1–9

Jesus said. "Sometimes bad things happen even to good people. But the important thing is that we keep trying to do God's will. We need to keep trying to change our ways. Let me tell you a story. There was a person who planted a fruit tree, but year after year it produced no fruit that one could eat. So it was decided to try for one more year giving it lots of TLC. If, after all that, it didn't yield a good crop, it was to be cut down."

Further Reflection

God certainly has been good to us. We owe everything we have to God. And in return all we're asked to do is to act right, or else we'll end up like the tree that wouldn't give any fruit. It's actually a pretty simple and practical rule for life.

Prayer

Dear God, sometimes I think I'm your gift to the world. I think every-one should take care of my needs before anything else. I really need to be pulling my own weight like everyone else has to do. It's the way life works. I don't need to try to make it work my way. Please help me to...

My Thoughts: David Klein

I don't see why Jesus told the story about the fruit tree. The story seems to contradict when he said about trying to do God's will even after some-thing bad happens. I would think the story would be more meaningful with the planter having faith in the tree and never cutting it down, even if it didn't bear fruit.

❧•☙

Fourth Sunday of Lent (Cycle A)

1 Samuel 16:6–7, 10–13

God said to Samuel, "I have chosen the one I want to be the king of my people. He is one of the three sons of Jesse. I want you to anoint him and crown him king." Samuel was very curious as to which of the three sons would be king, since God did not actually tell him which one it would be. Samuel said, "Is it the oldest son? He looks as though he would make a good king." God said, "No, Samuel, it is not the oldest. You can't judge a person by his appearance. He might not be the right person for the job. You must judge a person by what is in that person's heart. I want the youngest son David to be king."

David was just a very young man, who spent his time taking care of sheep, but Samuel did as God told him. That day he anointed and crowned David king of the people. He became a very good and wise king.

Psalm 23:1–6 *God is my shepherd.*

God takes care of all my needs. God watches over me. God gives me a home to live in. God gives me water to drink. God guides me along the right way. Even when I'm walking by myself in a strange place, I don't feel scared because I know God is with me. God has blessed me with many things. I can never repay God for the kindnesses I've been showered with.

Ephesians 5:8–14

St. Paul wrote a letter that said, There was a time in your life when you didn't know where you were going. That happened before Jesus became the light for the world. Now he shows all peoples and all of us what is good, what is just, and what is true. He shines light on our lives and shows us what to do. It seems, too, that if we are really followers of

Christ, we should become shining lights to all the people in the world so that they may know how to lead lives full of love.

John 9:1–41

One day while Jesus was walking through the streets of a city, he saw a very sad sight. He saw a young blind man begging for food. From looking at him it was obvious that the young man was born blind. Some people walking with Jesus asked, "Why is this man blind? Is it because his parents committed a serious sin, or did he himself do something bad? Is that why God is punishing him?"

Jesus was amazed at these questions and answered, "How could you even think that? God loves us. God doesn't punish people that way for committing sins. This man or his parents may never have committed a serious sin in their lives. You shouldn't judge that people are bad just because they look different from us."

Then Jesus said something that startled all of them. He looked them squarely in the eyes and said, "I am the light of the world." Bending down to the ground he spit in his hands and took some dirt and made mud out of it. He smeared mud all over the man's eyes. "Go and wash that mud off," Jesus said to the blind man.

When the blind man washed his face, he couldn't hold back his excitement, because for the first time in his life, he could see. The Jesus said to the people, "I was sent into this world to make people see not only with their eyes but also with their hearts. I have come to help people see how to live good lives."

Further Reflection

When I just think about myself and my own needs, my ego blinds me to the realities that are all around me of people in need of all sorts of help.

Prayer

Dear God, open my eyes and my heart to the needs of others. Please help me to…

My Thoughts: David Klein

I think the message from Samuel lives every day in our dealings with people. People today base too many judgments on the outward appearance and not enough on what's inside. We must surround ourselves with good-hearted people rather than good-looking people. I also think it is fitting that God anointed a shepherd because Jesus always talked of a shepherd's goodness in his lessons.

❧❧•❧❧

Fourth Sunday of Lent (Cycle B)

2 Chronicles 36:14–17, 19, 23

Many, many years ago, in fact a couple of thousand years ago, God's chosen people (including the leaders and priests) were living very wicked lives. They were so bad, they even did things in the house of God that no one should ever do for any reason. God wasn't very happy with the things that were going on, so messengers called prophets were sent to tell the people to clean up their acts. The people only laughed at God's messengers and kept living wicked lives. God got so mad that neighboring enemies were allowed to capture the whole country. The enemy burned everything in sight and took all the people away to be slaves. They went to a place called Babylon.

Then many years later, after a great battle, a new king took over most of the world. His name was Cyrus. God gave this new king the idea of rebuilding the destroyed city of Jerusalem and freeing the slaves. He called all the people together and said, "God has made me the ruler of most of the world. I feel I should repay God for the goodness I've received. I have decided to rebuild all of Jerusalem and especially that beautiful house of God which used to be there. Anybody who once lived there and wants to go back there has my permission to go. May God bless anyone who decides to help me."

Psalm 137:1–6 *How good God really is to us*

When we were prisoners we used to sit and cry because we still remembered when we were free. The people who captured us tried to make us be happy. They wanted us to sing songs. But how could we sing songs when we had nothing good to sing about? How could we sing songs when we were so sad? We were sad because we were not able to live in our own homes. It made us even sadder thinking about how happy we were when we were free. We didn't ever want to forget how happy we once were.

Ephesians 2:4–10

St. Paul wrote a letter that said, You know, God really is good to us. God sent us Jesus who taught us about "real life." In fact, God has been so good to us that a special place has been set aside for each of us when we die. God did all of this for us. We couldn't have done any of it by ourselves. God gave everything as a special gift to us. Even our very lives are special gifts from God. God gave us our lives so that we could live good lives full of kind actions.

John 3:14–21

One day Jesus was talking to a VIP whose name was Nicodemus. He said, "Nicodemus, God loves us and the whole world so much that God's only Son was sent to show everyone how to live. Everybody who listens to him and follows him will be happy living with God when they die. God didn't send the Son to earth to make life harder for everyone. God sent the Son to save us. It all seems very simple. God sent the Son to be an example for everyone to follow. God sent the Son to be a light to the world. Everybody who follows the light becomes a light for others. Those who sin all the time are not following the example of God's Son and so are not good examples for others to follow."

Further Reflection

God certainly works in wonderful ways. The Israelites were sent Cyrus to build the Temple. We were sent Jesus to build the kingdom. God provides for all times and all places and all peoples.

Prayer

Dear God, thank you for being you. Thank you for being in our lives and in our history. Please help me to...

My Thoughts: Kristin Nelson

These passages really show how good God is to us. Despite us constantly disappointing him and sinning, he still wants to bless us. You finish the prayer. I would say "...remember how merciful and great you are."

❧❧•❧❧

Fourth Sunday of Lent (Cycle C)

Joshua 5:9–12

God said to Joshua, "I have saved you from your slavery." And so while they were still out in the desert, the people celebrated the Passover. The next day there was enough food they could gather from the land that they didn't have to eat manna any more.

Psalm 34:2–7 *How wonderful God is*

Bless God always. We should glory in God's goodness. Let us praise God's name. We sought God and were helped.

2 Corinthians 5:17–21

St. Paul wrote a letter that said, If you are Christ's, you are a new creation. Through Christ we have been reconciled with God.

Luke 15:1–3, 11–32

The leaders were all talking behind Jesus' back because he was associating with sinners. So he told them this story. He said, "Once there was a man who had two sons. The younger one said. 'Give me right now the money you'd give me when you die. I want to get as far away from here as I can.' The father did.

"The son left and wasn't heard from for a long time. He squandered all that he had received from his father. At that time there was a terrible famine in the country. No one lifted a finger to help him so he got a job on a farm taking care of pigs. He wasn't given much to live on and wanted to eat the food he fed the pigs, but it was against regulations. Pretty soon he didn't have a cent to his name. He really was starving when he began to think about his own country. He thought to himself: 'My father's workers have plenty to eat. I'll go back home and beg my father to let me be one of his hired hands.' So he set out toward home.

"When he was still far off, his father saw him coming. Beside himself with joy, he ran to meet his son, threw his arms around him, kissed him, and wouldn't let him go. The son said, 'I've done so many wrong things. I don't deserve to be your son. Let me work for you as a hired hand.' The father would hear nothing of it. He had his servants clean him up and then they had a great welcome-home party for him.

"The older brother was out in the field when all this was happening and he got real mad when he heard what his father had done. He came in screaming, 'You've never done anything special for me or my friends. I've always been loyal to you. I worked hard all these years while he was out throwing all your money away. It's just not fair.' The father said, 'Look son. I've always had you with me. Everything I have is yours. I just had to celebrate since your brother is home with us. I was sure he was dead by now. He's really alive and has come back to us. This really makes me happy. I hope you can understand that.' "

Further Reflection

I've always been impressed how the father in this story of Jesus' never asks the son what he did, or where he was, or why he did what he did. He just willingly accepts the son back unconditionally. That's the feeling I get when I use the sacrament of reconciliation: total acceptance form a loving God.

Prayer

Dear God, I am so grateful to you for the many ways I experience you in my life, when I receive the sacraments of our faith. Please help me to...

My Thoughts: Tom Klein

I have always sided with the loyal son during my previous readings of this story. However, I have come to see the story in a new light—the father places true importance upon family and love rather than material possessions. This is a great lesson for all to learn, especially in today's increasingly materialistic world.

❧❧•❧❧

Fifth Sunday of Lent (Cycle A)

Ezekiel 37:12–14

God said, "Listen, my people. I will call you all back together. You have been scattered all over the earth, but I will bring you all back and make you one community again. I will make you a great nation and give your nation life. You will be a good and happy people once again."

Psalm 130:1–8 *God, give us life*

God, in my sinfulness I beg you to hear my prayers as I pray for forgiveness. If you don't, I wont be able to stand it. I'm trying to do better. God, I trust in you more than I trust in anybody else. You have always been true to your word. Give me back my life renewed.

Romans 8:8–11

St. Paul wrote a letter that said, To spell it out simply, there are two ways to live: you can be selfish and do things only for your own pleasure, or you can be a self-giving person helping others to live good lives. If you live the second way, then you have the spirit of Jesus in you, and you are a Christian.

John 11:1–45

Jesus was preaching to some people when he received a note from his friends Martha and Mary. The note said, "Dear Jesus, our brother Lazarus is very sick. We think he is going to die. Can you come quickly? We need you. Love, Martha and Mary."

Jesus was a long distance away. Before he got to their home, Lazarus died. In fact, when Jesus finally did get there, Lazarus had been buried for four days. Everybody was very upset because Lazarus had died so quickly and unexpectedly. Mary and Martha hadn't eaten or slept for days. When they saw Jesus they both ran into his arms and began to cry. They both were very upset. "Jesus," they said, "if you only could have been here sooner, maybe all of this wouldn't have happened." Jesus said, "Don't worry. Your brother will come to life again! I am the source of life. Anyone who believes in me will always have life." Jesus began to cry, too, because he felt very badly that Lazarus had died before he got there.

Then he said to them, "Will you take me to the tomb where you buried him?" When they got there Jesus said, "Move the stone away from the doorway of the tomb." Jesus prayed to God and shouted into the tomb, "Lazarus, get up and come out here." A few moments later Lazarus came out of the tomb. No one could believe the sight. All the people began to cry because they were so happy to have Lazarus back with them. And that night they had a wonderful party to celebrate.

Further Reflection

There are two ways to live: you can be selfish, or you can be self-giving. There's a little of both in all of us. Hopefully, the self-giving outweighs the selfishness.

Prayer

Dear God, today help me to think of others. Help me to place their needs before mine. Please help me to…

My Thoughts: David Klein

I would like to give more of myself. At times, I find myself acting put out when someone asks something of me. Later, I look back on my actions and wonder why I acted as I did and I feel guilty about it. I wish I could be more giving of myself without gaining something for myself in return.

❧❧•❧❧

Fifth Sunday of Lent (Cycle B)

Jeremiah 31:31–34

One day God said, "Pretty soon I'm going to make a covenant with my people. It won't be like the last one I made with their ancestors. They broke that one. This new covenant I make with my people will be written in their hearts and cherished. I will really be their God and they will really be my people. They will not have to teach people about me because everyone will already know me as their God. I will forgive everyone when they sin and then they will sin no more."

Responsorial Psalm 51:3–4,12–15 *God, forgive me*

Forgive me, God, because you are so good. Take away all of my sins. Don't just take away my sins but also take away the guilty feeling I have because I have sinned. Help me to be really good and make me feel like a new person all over. Stay with me always and give me the help of your Holy Spirit, too. Lord, let me feel the goodness of being saved by you and in return, I'll teach other sinners like myself how good you are.

Hebrews 5:7–9

Early in the Church, someone wrote a letter that said, When Jesus lived here on earth, he used to pray to God an awful lot. In fact, he prayed real hard. God always heard his prayers. God helped Jesus to do what he had to do and it was because Christ did this that he was able to save the world. He became our Savior!

John 12:20–33

Once some people from another country came up to one of Jesus' friends and said, "We're on a visit here. We're from out of the country. We've heard about Jesus and we'd like to talk to him if we can."

Jesus must have been doing some serious thinking because when he came out to meet these new people, he asked, "Have any of you ever noticed that unless a seed is planted in the earth and dies, it just stays a seed. But if it is planted and dies then it grows out of the ground as a new plant with a lot of fruit on it. It's sort of the same with people. If people just love themselves then they never really grow, but if people are willing to do anything for a friend, even die for that friend, then they are alive and really grow and will someday be happy with God forever. If any one of you believes what I am saying, then follow me. I have to admit that right now I'm a little scared about the future. I'd like to pray to God to change whatever's going to happen but I know God wants me to accept whatever is in store for me." Then he said a short prayer he used to say a lot: "God, I will praise your name forever and ever."

Further Reflection

Prayer is an important part of our lives. It's our way of talking to God about the things going on in our lives. Jesus did it and received a great deal from it.

Prayer

Dear God, you are always there helping and supporting me. May I keep a prayer to you on my lips always. Please help me to…

My Thoughts: Emily Miller

Prayer is a way of helping us through our problems. God will always be there to help us. Jesus prayed to God for help and he helped him. From his prayer, we are blessed.

❧❧•❧❧

Fifth Sunday of Lent (Cycle C)

Isaiah 43:16–21

God said, "Forget about the past. I'm doing something new for you right now. I will protect you and save you and help you right now. I'm not in the past. I'm here right now with you. You are the people I am forming for myself."

Psalm 126:1–6 *God has done great things for us*

We could hardly believe it when God freed us from slavery. God has done great things for us. For so long we cried every day. Now we are so happy and filled with joy.

Philippians 3:8–14

St. Paul wrote a letter that said, For Christ I have given up everything. Christ is my fortune. I hope I can be like Christ in all things, even his suffering. Life is like a race. I'm not yet on the last lap but I can see my goal, my finish line. I'm going to stay at it till I'm done.

John 8:1–11

One day while Jesus was out in the garden of Olives, a lot of people came around him. He took the opportunity to teach them a few things. In the middle of his talk some people brought a woman to him who was caught being unfaithful to her husband. They wanted to stone her like the law allowed, and they wanted Jesus to agree with them. He bent down and started writing something in the dirt. Then he stood up and said, "Let the one who is without sin throw the first stone." Embarrassed, they left one by one. Then he said to the woman, "There's no one here to condemn you, so you can go, but don't do that stuff again."

Further Reflection

Sometimes I can forget how forgiving God is to me. Sometimes I forget that I will be forgiven only to the extent that I forgive others.

Prayer

Dear God, I sure haven't the right to point fingers at anyone. I need to work on my own faults a lot more than I do. Please help me to…

My Thoughts: Jason Merkel

Dear God, throughout my life you have blessed me wonderfully. The love that you have shown me, my family, and friends: everything that is great in my life would not be had it not been for you. And yet I sin against you, and you welcome me back with forgiving embraces. Truly you are great. Help me, dear God, to love others as you have shown your love for me. Help me to spread your love and saving grace to all those in my life. Thank you so very much, dear God, thank you. Amen.

᪻᪻•᪻᪻

Passion Sunday (Palm Sunday)

Matthew 21:1–11

When Jesus got very close to the city of Jerusalem, his disciples found one of the best riding animals in the area for him. They borrowed it and made a saddle out of their cloaks. They helped Jesus get on the top of the animal and then had a parade into the city streets of Jerusalem. It was a marvelous parade. As Jesus passed by, the people threw tree branches and flowers down on the road. They waved at Jesus with their hands, and with colorful pieces of cloth and with palm branches they had cut down from nearby trees. After he passed they joined in the parade itself. They sang many happy songs. One of them was, "Hosanna to the Great One."

Isaiah 50:4–7

God chose me to do some special work. I am to tell the people about God's goodness no matter what the outcome. God will be there to help me say what needs to be said. It doesn't matter if people refuse to hear the truth.

Psalm 22:8–9, 17–20, 23–24 *God, you are my strength*

Everyone makes fun of me and scoffs at me for speaking the truth. They even mock me. They are out to get me. They want to condemn me and divide up my possessions among themselves. God, help me.

Philippians 2:6–11

St. Paul wrote a letter that said, Christ became human because God wanted him to show us how to really love. Christ didn't say "no." He gladly accepted what God wanted him to do. Jesus loved us so much he even died on a cross to save us from the slavery of sin. Christ is now Lord of all that is or ever will be.

Matthew 26:14—27:66

On the Thursday before he died, Jesus sat down with some of his friends to eat the holy Passover meal. They ate all the special foods that had been cooked for the feast. They talked about their ancestors being freed from slavery through God's help. They even sang many of their favorite old spirituals. During the meal Jesus took some bread off the table and blessed it. He passed it around the table and everyone broke off a piece to eat. As they were doing this Jesus said, "This is my body. Take and eat it." Then Jesus took a glass of wine, drank from it, and passed it around for his friends to drink. While they were drinking out of the cup, Jesus said, "Drink from this cup. This is a sign that we are sealing a new covenant of love and friendship. This is my blood."

Later on while they were still talking around the table, for some reason or other, some of the people got into an argument about who was the most important. Jesus stopped the argument by saying, "I don't think it's important at all whether any of you is *the* greatest or *the* best or *the* most powerful. I think what is most important is, Do you help and love other people? Are you willing to wait on other people and do whatever is possible to help other people in need? It is only when you are willing to help other people that you yourself can become a really great person." Jesus' friends were ashamed for the way they had been carrying on.

After the dinner was over, Jesus and a couple of his close friends went out into the garden to pray. (They often prayed together.) This time, after a few minutes of praying together, Jesus wanted to pray by himself. He said, "Why don't you all pray some more? I want to pray by myself for a while. I've got some things to think about. I'll go over there by that big rock to pray." Jesus then started to pray to God. "God, the going is getting kind of rough. I don't know if I can do all that you want me to do, but with your help I will be able to do whatever you want me to do."

While Jesus was praying, soldiers came into the garden, arrested him as a traitor of the government, and dragged him away. While Jesus was waiting to be brought before the judge, the soldiers who were guarding him punched him and slapped him in the face. They poked him with sticks, beat him, and called him all sorts of names.

Finally, Jesus was brought before a judge whose name was Pilate. Pilate asked Jesus some questions: "Are you a traitor? Do you tell people not to pay taxes? Are you a king?" Jesus would not answer any of the questions. Then Pilate called in his advisors and said, "We're going to have to let Jesus go free. None of the things he has been arrested for will hold up in court. We can't prove any of them. He's just not guilty of any crime." His advisors kept insisting that they wanted him crucified. Pilate didn't want to have any part of Christ's death so he said, "I'm washing my hands of this whole mess. I don't want to have anything more to do with this. Do whatever you want, but don't involve me."

They dragged Jesus away. They took him to the top of a nearby hill where they nailed him to a cross and let him hang there till he died. While he was hanging on the cross, they threw things at him and hit him with sticks and made fun of him. They said things like, "If you are the son of God, come down off the cross and save yourself." After about three hours, Jesus looked up to heaven and said, "God, I can do no more." Then his whole body went limp and he died. When the soldiers were sure that Jesus was dead, they took him down and buried him in a tomb that was nearby.

Further Reflection

In those few short days, Jesus experienced triumph coming into Jerusalem and total rejection on the cross of his death. He did all of it for us. He did it to show us how to live the way God wants us to live.

Prayer

Dear God, how blessed are we to have your son as our savior. He didn't just magically wave his hands and save us. He came to earth and lived among us as one of us. He showed us how you wanted us to treat one another. Please help me to always...

My Thoughts: Michael Fenton

I found Jesus' comment on the issue of who was the most important—"Do you help and love other people?"—to be the most striking. College has been difficult for me as I struggle to find a major and a future career or calling in life. Many times have I dreamt of becoming "the best" or the "most powerful." But I must always keep in mind the way God wants me to live and what it means to "become a really great person."

TWO

THE TRIDUUM
(THREE DAYS OF PRAYER)
AND EASTER SUNDAY

The Lord's Supper (Holy Thursday)

Exodus 12:1–8, 11–14

God said to Moses and Aaron, "I want you to celebrate a special meal before you leave on your journey from Egypt. Every family is to sacrifice a lamb and then spread some of its blood on the front of their doors. Then they are to cook and eat the lamb. If a given family is too small for this elaborate meal, let them join with another family close by. Disaster will come to any home that does not do this precisely. I want you to do this once a year from now on, no matter where you are."

Psalm 116:12–13, 15–18 *Do this in remembrance*

How shall I pay back God for all the good that I have received? I will do whatever God wants. I will call upon God's name. I will offer to God a sacrifice of praise and thanksgiving. I will serve God alone.

1 Corinthians 11:23–26

St. Paul wrote a letter that said, This is how we heard we were supposed to celebrate the Eucharist. Every time you do this you are proclaiming the death of Jesus until he comes again. On that special night, Jesus took some bread from the table, blessed it, broke it, and gave it to his friends, saying, "This is my body, given you for you." Later during the meal, Jesus took a cup of wine and said, "This is my blood of the new covenant. Drink this and remember me."

John 13:1–15

During supper Jesus got up from the table and poured some water into a bowl and then went around the table and washed the feet of all of his disciples. When Jesus came to Peter, there was a bit of a struggle. Peter didn't want Jesus to stoop down and wash his feet. When Jesus explained the symbolism, Peter wanted him to not only wash his feet, but his hands and his head as well. As he finished up, Jesus said to them all, "What I have done, you, too, must do. Be of service to others."

Further Reflection

In the time of Jesus, it was a wonderful gesture of hospitality to wash someone's feet when they came to your home. That was in the days of dirt roads and sandals. Hospitality is a good virtue to work on.

Prayer

Dear God, everything we know about your Son from Scripture is there to give us examples of how to live our own lives. I want to be a more giving person. Help me to...

My Thoughts: Steve Jaeger

Bathing ourselves...by blood? I'm searching for a connection between the passages. Are we to sacrifice ourselves and our self-proclaimed roles in life for God? The Bible says "yes."

ॐ•ॐ

Good Friday

Isaiah 52:13—53:12

He will be admired, in spite of his looks. At that point there was nothing physically appealing about him, yet he suffered for our sake. By his suffering, we were cleansed. He was badly treated yet willingly accepted it all. He gave his life that all might live.

Psalm 31:2, 6, 12–13, 15–17, 25 *God, I put my life in your hands*

God, you are my refuge. Help me. In your hands, I put my whole life. All my trust is in you. I put all my hope in you, too.

Hebrews 4:14–16, 5:7–9

Early in the Church, someone wrote a letter that said, Let us keep the faith because our belief is in Jesus the High Priest, who is like us in all things except sin. Let us ask and we will receive mercy and help.

John 18:1—19:42

One day Jesus went out into the park with his friends. It was a very beautiful park and they used to go there often. While they were in the park, Judas came near Jesus. He had some police with him. (Judas had been a good friend of Jesus but then turned against him.) When Jesus saw them he asked, "What do you want?" One of the police stepped forward and said, "We're looking for a person named Jesus." Jesus said, "Then I'm the one you're looking for." As they started to grab Jesus, Peter got very angry. He pulled out his sword and started to swing it at the people to scare them away. He ended up cutting off someone's ear before Jesus could say, "Peter, put your sword away. I don't want any violence."

The police arrested Jesus and dragged him off to court. Peter followed them and when they went into the courthouse, Peter stayed outside waiting to see what would happen. A woman came up to Peter and looked at him. She thought she had seen him somewhere before. Then she remembered and asked, "Aren't you a friend of the man Jesus whom they just took into court?" Peter was afraid, so he said, "I don't know what you're talking about!" She was sure he was lying, but she dropped the matter.

Inside the courtroom the judge was asking Jesus all kinds of questions about his friends and his work and where he lived. The judge couldn't find any crime that Jesus had committed, so he sent him to another court. While Jesus was being taken to the other court, some people asked Peter, "Are you sure you're not a friend of Jesus?" Peter shouted back, "No!" One of them said, "I'm sure you are his friend." Again Peter said, "No I'm not!" At that moment a rooster crowed. When Jesus got to the next court, the judge's name was Pilate. After asking Jesus many questions, Pilate couldn't find anything wrong that he had done either. However, he was afraid to just let Jesus go, so he made a deal with his advisors. Pilate said, "We'll give the people a choice. They can decide for themselves whether they want to let Jesus go free or that prisoner Barabbas that we've got locked up in our jail." Pilate was sure that they would let Jesus go. He took the two of them out on the front steps of the courthouse and asked the people to vote. He was shocked when they all shouted, "Free Barabbas! Free Barabbas!"

Pilate decided to have Jesus beaten up to see if that would satisfy the people, but when he brought Jesus back out to show them what he had done to him, they just kept chanting, "Kill him! Kill him! Kill him." Pilate was afraid to stand up to the unruly crowd, so he condemned Jesus to death and they dragged him away. They nailed Jesus to a cross and stood around waiting for him to die. It seemed like it took an awfully long time, but finally Jesus took one last breath and died. Afterward, a friend of Jesus' got permission to bury him in a nearby cemetery.

Further Reflection

This is the day Jesus died for our sins, died for *my* sins. Jesus loved me so much he was willing to die for me. In my gratitude I want to try to live the best I can.

Prayer

Dear God, you sent your Son to show us how to live. He did a good job. He was even willing to give up his life for us. Help me to show my gratitude by living my life in doing your will. Please help me to...

My Thoughts: Brian Melody

Having faith is one of the most important things in life. Jesus showed us throughout his lifetime that having faith in God will make life better. If we as humans trust other people and the Lord, we will benefit by living happier lives.

❧❧•❧❧

Easter Vigil

Genesis 1:1—2:2

In the very beginning, God created everything out of nothing. God said, "Let it be light out," and it was. Then God made the sky. After that, the oceans were next on the agenda. The continents were left where the water receded. All kinds of plants started to grow on the dry ground. The nights were lit by so many stars you couldn't count them all. Animals roamed around on the earth. All kinds of fish swam in the oceans. God created humans and put them in charge of everything. When everything was the way God wanted, a long rest was in order.

Psalm 104:1–2, 5–6, 10, 12–14, 24–25 *God, send us the Spirit to make everything new again*

Let us praise God for all the goodness we have received. God made the heavens and the earth and everything that is on it. God made the oceans, the land, the mountains, the birds, and the animals. The earth is full of God's goodness.

Genesis 22:1–18

Once a long time ago, there was a very good person whose name was Abraham. God wanted someone to become the founder of a great nation. God wanted to choose Abraham for the job, but God had to make sure that Abraham would do everything he was told to do, no matter what. God came up with a plan. "Abraham, I'm going to ask you to do something for me. It's going to be very difficult for you to do it. But this is what I want you to do. I want you to go up that mountain with your son Isaac. When you get to the top, I want you to sacrifice Isaac as an offering to me."

Abraham didn't want to do it, but he knew that if that's what God wanted, that's the way it had to be. So Abraham took his son for a walk up the mountain. When they got to the top they built a small altar. Then although he didn't want to do it, Abraham put his son on the altar as God had asked him to do. He was just about to stab a knife into Isaac's heart when a messenger from God appeared and said, "Wait! Don't do it! All God wanted to do was to test you. You passed. You don't have to kill your son."

Both Abraham and Isaac were very happy and relieved about that. They offered God another kind of sacrifice and then the messenger said, "Abraham, God is very pleased with the things you are doing. As a reward God wants you to be the founder of a great nation."

Psalm 16:5, 8–11 *God, I put all my hope in you*

God, you are the one who holds it all together for me. I always feel your presence. You will never be far from me. Show me the way so I will not stray too far.

Exodus 14:15—15:1

God said to Moses, "Lift up your staff and the seas will open up so you and your people can escape without being captured." Moses did as God had instructed and all the people got to the other side safely. The Pharaoh's people were in hot pursuit. They followed Moses' people into the dried-out seabed. When all his people were completely safe, Moses motioned to the parted sea and it all came back together and drowned all of the Pharaoh's people who were trying to catch up with Moses and his people.

(Psalm) Exodus 15:1–6, 17–18 *Praise God for God is good*

I will sing a song to God for we have been saved. God has been our savior. Pharaoh's people were finally stopped from harming us. God brought us to the Promised Land where we would be safe. God's reign is forever.

Isaiah 54:5–14

God is the beginning and the end. God is the Holy One who is your maker. You were once shunned but now you are God's delight. "I have always loved you," said God the Redeemer, "and will shower you with things beyond your wildest dreams."

Psalm 30:2, 4–6, 11–13 *God, you are my savior. I praise you for your goodness*

God, you saved me and brought me out of a really bad time in my life. I praise you for your goodness. Sometimes I'm sad but you bring me out of it. I can't stop thanking you for your goodness and kindness.

Isaiah 55:1–11

God asked, "Are you thirsty? Come and drink. Are you hungry? Come and eat. Don't worry about the cost. Come to me, and you will have life and have it to the fullest. Bask in the light of my unending covenant. Come to me before it is too late. You, who have sinned, come to me and I will forgive all quickly. Heed what I have to say, for I offer you life."

(Psalm) Isaiah 12:2–6 *God offers us refreshing waters of salvation*

God is my savior. I have nothing to fear or be afraid of. Everything I have comes from God. I proclaim God's name and praise it forever. I shout with joy to everyone about God's goodness.

Baruch 3:9–15, 32—4:4

Turn to God and find peace and wisdom and real life. In God are all the answers. There is no other like the God we worship. Turn to God and live.

Psalm 19:8–11 *God, yours is the way*

God's way is perfect. God's way can be trusted. God's laws are true. God's way is worth more than all the gold in the world.

Ezekiel 36:16–28

God said to me, "The people were dispersed and captured by other nations because they stopped living my covenant with them. The time has come when I will give them a change of heart and bring them back to their own land. They shall be my people once again."

Psalm 42:3, 5; 43:3–4 *God, I long for you*

God, when will I see you face to face? I've gone up to the temple of God to give praise and honor to the name of God most high. God, take me to your dwelling place that I might abide with you forever. It would be sheer joy to play for you on the harp forever.

Romans 6:3–11

St. Paul wrote a letter that said, When we were baptized we accepted the whole package: Christ living, dying, and rising to new life. If we followed Christ in living and accepting death willingly, then we will also share in his resurrection. Our old self has died to sin. Since we have died with Christ we are now alive with him too.

Psalm 118:1–2, 16–17, 22–23 *Praise God in all things*

Let's give thanks to God for all the goodness we have received. God is truly merciful. We shall not die, but live. Wonderful and great is God.

Matthew 28:1–10 (Cycle A)

Sunday morning Mary Magdalene and some of the women came to finish the burial rites for Jesus. When they got to the tomb, they found that the stone in front of the entrance had been moved. When they went in, they saw a young man dressed in white sitting near where Jesus had been placed. They didn't see the body anywhere. The man said, "Don't be surprised. He's risen from the dead. Go tell the disciples that he will meet them in Galilee." As they left, Jesus appeared to them and said, "Peace." The women embraced him. "Don't be afraid," he said, "Go and tell the disciples to meet me in Galilee."

Mark 16:1–8 (Cycle B)

Sunday morning Mary Magdalene and some of the women came to finish the burial rites for Jesus. When they got to the tomb they found that the stone in front of the entrance had been moved. When they went in, they saw a young man dressed in white sitting near where Jesus had been placed. They didn't see the body anywhere though. The man said, "Don't be surprised. He's risen from the dead. Go tell the disciples that he will meet them in Galilee." The women left and because they were so frightened, they told no one.

Luke 24:1–12 (Cycle C)

Sunday morning some of the women came to finish the burial rites for Jesus. When they arrived at the tomb, they found that the stone in front of the entrance had been moved. When they went in, they saw two individuals in radiant clothes standing near where Jesus had been placed. They didn't see the body anywhere. One of the individuals said, "Don't look for Jesus here. He's risen from the dead. He's alive." The women went back to the other disciples and told them everything they had heard and seen. It was all too much to believe. So Peter went out to the tomb to see for himself.

Further Reflection

This whole liturgy tells us that throughout history God has always been there, loving and supporting and caring for us. What a blessing it is to be alive, and to know this is how it all happened.

Prayer

Dear God, you have been so good to me in the short time I have been alive on this earth. I am grateful for all you have given to me. I cherish the faith that has been handed down to me from people who centuries ago felt your presence in their lives. Please help me to…

My Thoughts: Steve Jaeger

When you look at the history of Christianity and Judaism alone, how can anyone even consider the idea that God does not exist? So much has happened, so much has been seen, so much has been recorded—and there's so much mystery behind it. It makes sense to me.

❧•❧

Easter Sunday

Acts 10:34, 37–43

Peter spoke to the people: "I'm telling you everything that I know about the life and death and rising of Jesus. He lived a good life, showing us how to live. We know God was with him. He was killed but then he rose on the third day after his death. We've got eyewitnesses who actually talked and ate with him after he came back from the dead. If you believe, you will be freed from your sins."

Psalm 118:1–2, 16–17, 22–23 *Jesus is risen. Alleluia*

God is good to us. God is great. God is everything to us. The one who was rejected has become our foundation. God has done marvelous things.

Colossians 3:1–4

St. Paul wrote a letter that said, Keep your sights high. Place your hope in the risen Jesus. Then when he comes again, you will share in his glory forever.

John 20:1–9

Early Sunday morning, Mary Magdalene went out to the cemetery where Jesus was buried. The stone in front of the tomb was moved, so she went and told Peter what she had seen. Peter and John went out to see for themselves. John outran Peter but waited until he got there. They went in the opened tomb and found only the wrappings there. Jesus was nowhere to be seen.

Further Reflection

What a thrill it must have been to discover that Jesus had truly risen from the dead. Their sadness was turned to joy. What a great day this is for us. All that Jesus taught us in his lifetime was confirmed in his rising from the dead. Truly he is the Son of God most high.

Prayer

Dear God, what blessings you have showered us with. Today is a celebration of the greatest gift you have given us. Today we rejoice in the rising of your Son from the dead, assuring us a place with you in your kingdom. Please help me to…

My Thoughts: Becky Musolf

Easter is a great celebration when we remember Jesus rising from the dead. It is a huge symbol of our faith in God. Sometimes I feel this gets lost in society with all the Easter bunny hype. Although, much of Easter is still about Christ rising, I think there needs to be even more emphasis on the religious aspect of the holiday, rather than on what the bunny left in our basket. This was truly one of God's miracles and shows we all have a place in heaven.

THREE
SUNDAYS OF THE EASTER SEASON

[Note: Easter Sunday itself is "technically" the first Sunday of Easter, which is why this section begins with the "second" Sunday of Easter.]

Second Sunday of Easter (Cycle A)

Acts 2:42–47

In the earliest days, everyone who belonged to the Church lived together in small communities. They also shared in common everything they had. They went to church together. They ate together. They prayed together. If they needed something, they would buy it out of their common fund. Everyone looked after one another. This kind of living seemed to catch on because every day they would have new members joining their communities.

Psalm 118:2–4, 13–15 *Let's give thanks to God*

Let everyone know that God's love lasts forever. Let everyone in the streets and at work know it. When I was in trouble, God helped me. I was given the strength and the courage to make difficult and serious decisions. With God's help, every day is worth living. God is so good to us.

1 Peter 1:3–9

St. Peter wrote a letter that said, God has been good to us and saved us. We've been made children of God. We have so much to be thankful for. Taking some of the hard lumps in life is easier when we know that in spite of everything, Jesus still loves us and helps us.

John 20:19–31

The week after Jesus was killed, his friends were still afraid of what might happen to them if they went out on the streets, so they locked themselves in a room. They wanted to hide out until people began to forget about Jesus. While they were hiding, Jesus appeared to them. He calmed their nerves by saying, "Peace to all of you." Then he talked to them for a while about different things. After they felt more relaxed, he said to them, "You know that God sent me to do a job. I was to spread the message of God's love and salvation to all, and now I want you to continue my work. I will send you the Holy Spirit who will give you the strength and courage and wisdom to preach this good news."

Further Reflection

Love, salvation, getting along with one another, sharing—these are all words central to the message Jesus was trying to share with us. He even promised to send the Holy Spirit to help us. When will we catch on?

Prayer

Dear God, you have been so good to me. Everything I have comes from you. Help me not only to live Christ's message but also to share that message with others. Please help me to…

My Thoughts: Kristin Nelson

These readings all remind me how it is that we were made to serve one another. We are not meant to hide away from others, and though it may be easier than dealing with people, it is not how we are. I can completely relate to the apostles in the third reading, wanting to be silent about my faith but that is not what God wants. The last statement in "Further Reflection" couldn't be truer: when will we catch on? We know what God wants or commands, yet we do differently.

❧❧•❧❧

Second Sunday of Easter (Cycle B)

Acts 4:32–35

In the old days everyone who believed in Jesus lived together as one happy family. They shared everything they had together. Nobody ever kept anything just for his or her own use. They shared their food, their clothes, their homes, their money, and their talents with one another. One of the rules they lived by was, if you need something and we have it, then you can use it. The people always looked out for the other person.

Psalm 118:2–4, 13–15, 22–24 *God's love lasts forever*

Let everyone in school know that God's love lasts forever. Let everyone on the streets know that God's love lasts forever. Let everyone who works know that God's love lasts forever. Let everyone who needs help know that God's love lasts forever. When I was having a rough time in school and was failing, God helped me to study. And later in life God gave me strength and courage to make many difficult and serious decisions. God has always helped and loved me. With God's help, every day is a beautiful day worth living. Let us be happy and glad, for God has been very good to us.

1 John 5:1–6

St. John wrote a letter that said, You know, of course, that everyone who believes in Jesus Christ is a child of God. Everyone who really loves God keeps the commandments. Everyone who is a child of God has the power to conquer the world because the power God gives us is our faith. Let me say that again. Whoever believes in Jesus is a child of God and has the power to conquer the world. It was Jesus who saved us by the water of baptism and by giving up his life for us. We know all of this because God's Holy Spirit, who speaks only the truth, told us so.

John 20:19–31

The week after Jesus was killed, his friends were still afraid of what might happen to them if they went out on the streets, so they locked themselves in a room. They wanted to hide out until people began to forget about Jesus. While they were hiding, Jesus appeared to them. He calmed their nerves by saying, "Peace to all of you." Then he talked to them for a while about different things.

After they felt more relaxed, he said to them, "You know that my Father in heaven sent me to do a job. I was to spread the message of God's love and salvation to all men, and now I want you to continue my work. I will send you the Holy Spirit who will give you the strength and courage and wisdom to preach this good news."

That day everyone was there to see Jesus except the apostle named Thomas. When the other apostles tried to tell Thomas about seeing Jesus, he said, "I don't believe a word you're saying. You're making the whole thing up. I won't believe Jesus appeared to you until I see him with my own eyes and touch him with my own hands."

About a week later all the apostles, including Thomas, were together when Jesus came to talk to them again. He said, "Peace be with all of you." Then he turned to Thomas and asked, "You see me, don't you? Come over here and touch me." Thomas was very scared but he answered back, "My Lord and my God." Looking at Thomas, Jesus said, "Thomas, you believed in me only after you saw me. There are going to be millions of people in the world who will believe in me even though they will never have the opportunity to see me as you have." Then Jesus left his friends.

St. John, who wrote this gospel, then added, P.S. You might be interested to know, as I come to the end of writing this book, that everything I put in this book was put there to help you believe in Jesus and his way of life.

Further Reflection

I'm a little like Thomas before and after. Sometimes I'm skeptical of religious matters and sometimes my faith overflows.

Prayer

Dear God, help my unbelief. Strengthen my faith. Please help me to...

My Thoughts: Angela Becker

Please help me to always know that God is in my presence and there to help and guide me. Help my faith be strong enough to overcome any doubts that I may have.

❧•❧

Second Sunday of Easter (Cycle C)

Acts 5:12–16

As the days went on, more and more people came together and joined the ranks of the early Christian Church. Peter had such a powerful reputation that they would lay sick people out on the road where he would pass just so his shadow would touch them.

Psalm 118:2–4, 13–15, 22–24 *God is truly good to us*

God's mercy is forever. God has always been there to help me. My salvation comes from God. This is truly a day God has made. Rejoice and be glad.

Revelation 1:9–13, 17–19

St. John wrote, I'm writing to you from exile because I preached about Jesus our Lord. I've had a vision. I was told to write what I saw so that you, too, might believe.

John 20:19–31

One Sunday night Jesus appeared to the disciples and the first thing he said was, "Peace be with you. As I was sent, so I am sending you." Thomas wasn't there when this happened. He didn't believe a word the other apostles said when they were relating it to him.

So a week later Jesus came back. This time he said to Thomas, "Touch my wounds so you will see that it is really me." Thomas did and then he said, "My Lord and my God." Jesus said to Thomas: "You believe because you saw that it is true. There will be people who will come after you who won't have the chance to see me in the flesh, but they'll believe in me anyway. They'll really make a leap of faith."

All of this has been handed down to us so that we might believe, too.

Further Reflection

Sometimes I don't think much about my faith. But it really comes home to me when I realize that most of the early Christians were actually killed because they believed in Jesus. It puts a different perspective on how easy my life and my beliefs are for me. They're something I really shouldn't take for granted.

Prayer

Dear God, what a blessing I've received from the traditions that have been handed down to me from the times of the apostles. My prayer is one of gratitude for the goodness you have showered on me. Please help me to…

My Thoughts: Chris Keyser

In today's world, we have been accustomed to believing only what seems real: that which we can touch and feel. Sometimes, putting hope and trust into something indirectly tangible can become very difficult. This is why we call our love and hope for God *faith*. If we trust in the Lord that our time spent on earth is only temporary and that another life with him awaits us, present times become much clearer.

❦

Third Sunday of Easter (Cycle A)

Acts 2:14, 22–28

After receiving courage from the Holy Spirit, Peter stood in front of a large crowd that had gathered on a street corner. He shouted, "Listen to me, all of you. I've got something important to say. What I have to say has given meaning to my life, and I'm sure it will help you, too. Jesus, the man who was killed about a month ago, was actually sent by God to save us and show us how to live. While he was alive he worked many wonderful miracles and gave us many wise sayings to live by. After he was killed, God raised him from the dead to prove that what he said and did was true. I have seen him since he came back to life, and so have many other people. You can ask them yourselves if you want to. His words and his example have changed my life. I hope that what I have been saying to you today has convinced you to follow Jesus, too."

Psalm 16:1–2, 5, 7–11 *God, show me the path to life*

God, I look to you for help and comfort. You have always stood by me when things got too rough to handle. Every day and night I kneel down and thank you for helping. I know that no real harm can come to me with you at my side. It makes me happy to know that you love me.

1 Peter 1:17–21

St. Peter wrote a letter that said, Whenever you plan on doing something, you should keep in mind that Jesus Christ saved us. He didn't save us by merely paying a large sum of money. He saved us by giving his life for us. By doing that, he gave us an example to help us to live good lives.

Luke 24:13–35

One day, when the news that Jesus had risen from the dead was still the main topic of every conversation, two of Jesus' friends were going out to dinner. Needless to say, they were talking together about the facts Peter and John had given them concerning Jesus being raised from the dead.

While they were walking along, a stranger who was walking in the same direction overheard some of their conversation. (The stranger was actually Jesus but the two friends didn't recognize him.) He was curious to hear what they were saying, so he said, "Excuse me, but I couldn't help overhearing some of your conversation. What are you two so excited about?" The two friends told him all about the incredible but true story of Jesus from beginning to end. As the three of them walked along together, one thing led to another and the two friends invited the stranger to eat dinner with them.

When they were seated around a table in the restaurant, a waiter brought over a basket of bread. Jesus picked up the bread, blessed it, and gave a piece to each of the two friends. When Jesus did this, their mouths dropped open and they were speechless. Their faces turned bright red, because it was only after talking with him for about two hours that the two friends finally realized that they were talking to Jesus himself. They couldn't wait to tell Peter and John and their other friends all about meeting Jesus. In fact, they were so excited that they didn't sleep a wink.

Further Reflection

It's kind of interesting. When we share a meal with others, we get to know them so much better.

Prayer

Dear God, I not only get to know your son better at the Eucharist, I get to know and love the people around me more. Please help me to…

My Thoughts: Becky Musolf

These passages remind me that Easter is not a sad time of the year, but it is rather a celebration of Christ's love for us, and even in the end he will be at our sides to calm our fears and reassure us that everything will be okay. He gave up so much for us.

❧❧•❧❧

Third Sunday of Easter (Cycle B)

Acts 3:13–15, 17–19

One day Peter was talking to a group of people. He was trying to explain some things about Jesus to them. He said, "You know, God, the God of our ancestors, raised Jesus from the dead. I'm telling you the truth. I saw him after he was raised from the dead and so did a lot of other people. I can give you their names if you want them. The evidence is too startling not to believe it. This should be enough to make you change your lives and turn to God to have your sins taken away."

Psalm 4:2, 4, 7–9 *God, please answer my prayer*

When I pray to you, God, please answer me. It's you who have always helped me before when I was in trouble. Please be kind to me and answer my prayers. I know that you help people who really believe in you. I really believe in you so please help me. God, be near me and let my heart be filled with true happiness. God, it is only when I know that you are very near to me that I am able to get a decent night's sleep. It is only when I know that you are very near me that I am really able to sleep peacefully.

1 John 2:1–5

St. John wrote a letter that said, My dear close friends, I am writing this letter to encourage you to live good lives. Sometimes we all commit sins. But always remember that Jesus, who is our go-between with God, frees us from our sins. In fact, he frees everyone from sin who wants to be freed. The only thing we really have to do is keep the commandments. Anyone who says, "I believe in Jesus," but doesn't keep the commandments is a liar. If any one of you really keeps the commandments Jesus gave us, then you will have the love of God in your heart.

Luke 24:35–48

One night when Jesus' friends were all together, they were listening to the story of how Jesus appeared to two of his friends while they were traveling toward the city of Emmaus. While they were all talking together Jesus came and stood in the middle of them. He said, "I wish that the peace of God is with all of you." They were very scared because they thought they were seeing a ghost.

He said to them, "Don't be afraid. It's only me. Come over here and touch me. If I were just a ghost, I wouldn't have real flesh and bones, would I?" They were so happy once they were sure it was really Jesus that they offered him some of the food they were eating. When they were more relaxed, he started talking to them seriously. He said, "I want you all to go out and preach to all the people you see that they are to be sorry for their sins and that I will save them all. I want you to start in Jerusalem and then go all over the world."

Further Reflection

Talking about Jesus is something I need to do more of because he has been such a positive force in my life.

Prayer

Dear God, give me the courage to talk openly about what Jesus has done for me. Please help me to...

My Thoughts: Joe Curry

In a time where talking about religion among acquaintances is sometimes a taboo topic, please help me to be true to myself. Please guide me to express my thoughts and concerns in words rather than in silence.

Third Sunday of Easter (Cycle C)

Acts 5:27–32, 40–41

When the apostles were in court the judge said, "I told you not to be preaching about Jesus and you've disobeyed me." Peter answered, "We feel it's better to do what God wants us to do, rather than listen to what you tell us to do." The judge was not pleased with the way Peter talked to him.

Psalm 30:2, 4–6, 11–13 *God, you mean everything to me*

God, you have always been my help. I sing your praises and shout to you with joy and gladness. Be my helper and my joy.

Revelation 5:11–14

St. John wrote, I had a vision. I saw God's throne and a lot of things going on around it. There were so many people there I couldn't count them all. Everyone and everything was shouting all kinds of praises to God.

John 21:1–19

One evening Peter and his friends went fishing. They caught nothing, even though they fished all night long. Early in the morning Jesus was standing on the shore and called out, "Throw your nets off the other side of the boat." As soon as he said that, John recognized who it was and shouted so everyone could hear, "It's Jesus." Peter was so excited he jumped overboard and swam to shore. The others came back to shore in the boat.

When they landed on shore, Jesus had already started to cook them something to eat on an open fire. After they finished eating, Jesus said to Peter, "Peter, do you love me?" "Of course I do," Peter answered back. "Then feed my lambs." Jesus asked the same question a second time. Peter answered the same way too. Jesus said, "Then take care of my sheep." After a third time with the same question Peter got a little perturbed. He replied, "Jesus, you know everything. You know that I love you." "Then feed my flock," Jesus answered. "When you were young you went and did what you wanted. When you get a little older, they will tie you up and carry you off." Jesus said this to kind of warn Peter about the way he was going to die.

Further Reflection

Jesus seems to be telling Peter with his same three questions to really look after the people who believe in him, no matter what. We're all called to look after those around us, basically because we are really all part of one family. (Jesus would say, one flock).

Prayer

Dear God, sometimes I like to just look out for myself. Sometimes I forget there are other people who really could use my help and concern. Please help me to...

My Thoughts: Joe Curry

In our increasingly independent and fast-paced society, it is easy to overlook those around us. We are preoccupied by our thoughts as we are rushing to our destination. I think even the simple gesture of a warm smile would show my concern for the many faces that I pass each day. Please help me to be more perceptive toward those around me so that I may offer help to those in need and brighten the days of those I encounter.

❧☙ ● ❧☙

Fourth Sunday of Easter (Cycle A)

Acts 2:14, 36–41

Peter got up in front of a large crowd of people and shouted at the top of his voice so that everyone could hear him: "I know and believe that Jesus Christ is the Lord and Savior of us all!" When the people heard him shouting, they all stopped talking and listened to what he had to say. Naturally they had a lot of questions to ask him when he had finished talking. The first question asked was, "If we believe in Jesus, what do we have to do?"

Peter had a quick answer because he had been asked that question many times before. He said, "You must change the way you live. You must reform. You have to stop sinning. You must love and help other people. You must be baptized as a sign to all that you really believe and want to live good lives. If you do all of this, God will send you his Holy Spirit to help you."

Psalm 23:1–6 *God is my shepherd*

God watches over me and takes care of all my needs. God gives me a home to live in. God gives me water to drink. God gives meaning to my life. Even when I'm walking by myself in a strange place, I don't feel scared because I know that God is with me to help me and give me courage. God gives me food to eat. I always have enough to drink. God has blessed me with many things. I will never be able to repay God for the kindnesses I've been showered with.

1 Peter 2:20–25

St. Peter wrote a letter that said, Christ came to earth that he might be an example for you. He hoped that one day you might follow in his footsteps. He never did anything wrong that people could point to. He never lied or cheated. He had nothing to hide or cover up. If someone hurt him or called him names, he never tried to get even. He loved everyone he met. What he wants you to do is to follow his example.

John 10:1–10

One day Jesus was trying to make an important point with his friends. He gave them a few examples to make what he was saying a little clearer. Jesus said, "Have you ever noticed that when a father comes home from work, he uses his key to unlock the door and comes in the front door and shouts to his wife and kids, 'Hi. I'm home!' The family runs to him and kisses him because they are happy to have him home. He spends the whole day working so that the family will have enough food to eat and enough clothes to wear. He comes home at night to love his family and to protect them and sometimes to help them with homework. If necessary, a father would even die to help his family. The family loves to have their father home."

Jesus kept talking: "Have you ever heard stories about a thief who breaks into a house by climbing in a back window? If the people are home, he almost scares them to death. Sometimes a burglar will beat up the people and lock them in the closet. All he is interested in is stealing money and valuable goods. It's very scary and frightening to have a robber in your home."

Jesus then said to his friends, "I am like the father who loves his family. There is nothing a good father wouldn't do for his family. I want you to know that there is nothing that I wouldn't do for you because I love you all very much. You should try to be that way too."

Further Reflection

Jesus' words are very powerful. He wants us all to live and act like he did. He wants us to have the love a parent has for a child in the family. That's unconditional love. That's powerful.

Prayer

Dear God, I want to be more like your Son. I need all the help I can get. Please help me to...

My Thoughts: Gina Glow

WOW! This is such a hard and yet such a wonderful meditation to reflect on. I try to live my life like Christ but whenever I mess up, all I can see is my imperfection. God is so good and I wish that sometimes I acted more like Christ. I try to and am getting better at it, but we are human and make mistakes. No matter what I think, we should all try to be living examples of Christ because it will not only please God but make the world a better place.

❧❧•❧❧

Fourth Sunday of Easter (Cycle B)

Acts 4:8–12

One day after Peter had been arrested, he was being questioned by some officials about his beliefs. He felt the Holy Spirit inside him and he said, "Some of you probably have seen us cure a lot of sick people. Some of them could not walk and we gave them the strength to walk. Some could not see and we gave them back their sight. We didn't do any of these things by ourselves. It was only because Jesus himself gave us the power that we are able to help other people. A lot of people didn't believe in Jesus and that is why he was killed. But we believed in Jesus and that is why he gave us this power to help people."

Psalm 118:1, 8–9, 21–23, 26, 27, 29 *God is good*

Let us thank God, for God is good to us. God will always be good to us. God is the only one we really can trust in. You can trust God more than anyone else in the world. God, I thank you for your kindness. You always answer me. You are the one who saved me. Even though other people forget you, I won't because I know that you have made everything that is wonderful in the world. God, I thank you for your kindness. You always answer my prayers. You are the one who saved me. I can never stop thanking you for your goodness toward me.

1 John 3:1–2

St. John wrote a letter that said, Do you have any idea how much God loves us? Because of God's goodness we can call ourselves God's children and that is what we are. A lot of people don't understand or recognize us for what we are because they never really understood or recognized Jesus either. We know we are children of God. We know that in the future when we see God face to face we will recognize God as the one who created us.

John 10:11–18

One day Jesus was talking to his friends about some serious things. He told them a story, something like this one: "Have you ever known anyone who owned a bunch of dogs? I did. This man really loved his dogs. He took care of them. He fed them. He took them for walks every day. He even gave them baths when they needed them. They were very happy dogs and the man loved them very much. This man loved those dogs so much he would rather die than let someone hurt them. He never let anyone else take care of the dogs because he knew that others did not love the dogs as much as he did, and so they wouldn't get as good care as he gave them."

There's a good lesson in this story for all of us. I try to be like that man even with my friends. I try to love them and help them and make them happy. There's nothing I wouldn't do for a friend. I'd even give my life for a friend.

Further Reflection

I like to think that I would give my life for a friend if it ever came to that. But since that probably will never happen, I still need to be the best friend I can be now.

Prayer

Dear God, help me to treat others as I would like to be treated. Please help me to...

My Thoughts: Nicole Borchardt

Help me to recognize how much you love me, and that no matter what I do, you will still love me that much. Thank you for loving me despite my faults and the stupid things I do. Help me to learn to love others, even when they drive me crazy. Please give me the patience that is necessary to love those who seem unbearable, and teach me to see Jesus in all of them, so that I would be able to lay my life down for them, if it came to that.

❧❧•❧❧

Fourth Sunday of Easter (Cycle C)

Acts 13:14, 43–52

Paul and Barnabas taught in the synagogue at Antioch. Many people listened and believed what they had to say. The next week when they came back some of the people didn't want them to come into the synagogue because they didn't want to hear what Paul and Barnabas were saying. Paul said, "We teach what has been handed down to us. If you don't want to listen, there are others who will. We'll even preach to the Gentiles because we believe that they are children of the one true God too." The people really got mad at what Paul was saying so they ran the two of them out of town.

Psalm 100:1–2, 3, 5 *We are God's people*

Sing to God joyfully. Serve God willingly. Come before God's throne humbly. God made us. We are God's. God is so wonderful and good.

Revelation 7:14–17

St. John wrote, I had a vision and saw a huge crowd so big you couldn't count them all. They were all around the throne. They willingly served God all day long.

John 10:27–30

Jesus said, "My followers know me and I know them. I have eternal life to share with them. I will protect them always. God will make sure of that. Actually God and I are one."

Further Reflection

The early Church started teaching some radical things. The people up until then believed there were two types of people, the people of God and those Gentiles. Paul and Barnabas started teaching that all people are really children of God. It's a lesson sometimes even I forget when I feel I'm better than other people.

Prayer

Dear God, there's so much hatred and jealousy and mistrust in this world. Give me your grace not to add to it. Please help me to...

My Thoughts: Kortney Jendro

We are a people who fracture things. There are new splinters forming every day. What I'm hoping we discover is that our names for "God" are interchangeable. Jesus, Yahweh, God, Allah—people who follow Buddha or Mohammed—these are just NAMES. As long as the faith is there, it does not matter how you pronounce it. These days we judge "spelling" too harshly.

❧❧•❧❧

Fifth Sunday of Easter (Cycle A)

Acts 6:1–7

In the early days of the Church when all the Christians lived together in communities, the workload got to be too much for the apostles. Peter called the other apostles and said, "In the past couple of months so many new people have joined our group that there's just too much work for the twelve of us to do alone. We can't buy all the food and make up the work lists and babysit the small children and earn extra money and make sure everybody's healthy and do the dishes and preach every day and baptize people every Sunday. It's just getting to be too much work. We've got to figure out a better way to divide up the work."

One of the other apostles said, "Why don't we pick a couple of other people who would be willing to supervise and see that certain work gets done? We could get someone to take care of the money, and someone to buy the food, and someone to buy all the clothing, and someone to take care of the repairs on the houses, and someone to watch all the children. We could also have a sign-up list for each of those jobs so that other people could help out too. That way the work load would be lighter and we could spend more time preaching and baptizing." They decided to try that plan because it sounded pretty good, and it worked out nicely. Everyone was very happy and even their preaching got better.

Psalm 33:1–2, 4–5, 18–19 *God, we know your way is right*

Let's praise God, for that's the way it should be. Let's make up some songs to sing to God. You can always trust what God tells you. God's kindness and goodness can be seen everywhere in the world. God loves those who are kind. God helps them when they are in need.

1 Peter 2:4–9

St. Peter wrote a letter that said, You are a special group of people. You have accepted Jesus as the example in life to follow. You do things differently from other people. You even act differently from other people. Other people can't figure out why you love everyone. To them that's stupid and ridiculous. But then, they don't believe in Jesus Christ as you do.

John 14:1–12

One day after Jesus rose from the dead, he was talking to some of his friends. He said, "I'm not going to be around much longer. Soon I'm going to go back to God in heaven. I hope I have been with you long enough for you to have learned that I am the way to truth and happiness. If you follow the way I have lived my life, you will find all the happiness you have ever wanted and more. If you follow my way of life, you will be able to do even greater things than I have. And because I'm leaving soon, you will be able to teach many more people the right way to live than I have ever had a chance to teach."

Further Reflection

There are lots of people in our lives that we take for granted. They aren't going to be around all the time. I should savor their love and friendship and let them know it, before it's too late.

Prayer

Dear God, you've showered me with so many wonderful people in my life. Help me to not take them for granted. Please help me to…

My Thoughts: Steve Jaeger

It's a wonder that there are so many people in the world. Every single one is different and unique, and there never has been nor will there be any two identically alike. Anyone who has experienced the death of a loved one can relate to the preciousness of life and how important it is to tell someone that you love him or her. Every person is a gift from God, and we learn from people. We are, by nature, instruments of teaching and continually learning. On a rock-bottom level, we are instructed by everyone we meet. Always thank your teachers.

❧•❧

Fifth Sunday of Easter (Cycle B)

Acts 9:26–31

Right after Saul became a Christian, he went to Jerusalem to join the group of Christians living there. But the people there were afraid of him because they thought he was still going around killing Christians. They didn't really believe he was converted. When Barnabas, a friend of Saul's, saw that the people didn't want to have anything to do with him he tried to explain how Saul had changed his ways of living. He told them how Saul had seen the Lord and then became a Christian. They finally accepted Saul and listened to him. But one day he was almost killed by some people who were arguing with him, so he got out of town and went to work in another Christian community where everyone accepted him and liked him.

Psalm 22:26–27, 28, 30, 31–32 *God is my support*

I will do what I have to do with God at my side. Anyone else who wants God to help should praise God. They will be happy. They will get what they need. Those who are humble and good will praise God. Everyone all over the earth will pray to God. Every different nation of people will pray to God. God will be the only one they will all pray to. I will do whatever God wants. All my family that comes after me will, too. I will teach my children about God and God's goodness so that they can teach their children and their children's children.

1 John 3:18–24

St. John wrote a letter that said, Do you know what I'd like everyone to do? I'd like to see everyone stop just talking about loving other people and start really loving other people! It's the only way we can really prove that we are following Christ. This is the only way we'll be at peace with God and with ourselves. It's not such a hard thing to love other people. We know God will give us all the help we'll need. That's the only thing God really asks us to do: Love one another. It's the least we can do.

John 15:1–8

One day Jesus said something like this to some of his close friends: "A couple of days ago I was watching a friend of mine while he was watering some tomato plants he owns. He takes really good care of them, watering them, seeing that they get enough sunlight, keeping the bugs away from them, and cutting off the old dead leaves. They are the most beautiful tomato plants I have ever seen. And you should see the great tomatoes he has. Watching him got me to thinking about God. God is sort of like my friend. I'm kind of like the tomato plant. God takes care of me real well. You are all like the branches with the tomatoes on them. If you stick with me, God will take good care of you too. And you'll all bear much fruit."

Further Reflection

Love is such an easy thing to talk about, and such a hard thing to live out in my life.

Prayer

Dear God, give me your help because I really have a hard time loving some people. Please help me to…

My Thoughts: Steve Jaeger

The reflection of 1 John 3:18–24 was a good change of pace. It expressed more personal passion than translation. The reflection of John 15:1–8 made the reading more up-to-date, simple, and less threatening than the Bible passages. Feelings of passion and welcoming were clearly seen in the set of reflections. The general theme I read from this is to care for others and for God because God already cares a great deal for us.

❧❀❧

Fifth Sunday of Easter (Cycle C)

Acts 14:21–27

Paul and Barnabas went all over preaching and encouraging the people to place and keep their faith in Jesus and his way.

Psalm 145:8–13 *God, we praise your name everywhere and all the time*

God has always been good to us. God has always been kind. Let's tell everyone how good God is.

Revelation 21:1–5

St. John wrote, I had a vision. I saw what it was like at the end of time. God and all the people of the earth were living together in peace and happiness. All things were made new.

John 13:31–35

Jesus said, "My time is almost up. I won't be with you much longer. Remember what I've taught you. Love one another."

Further Reflection

What a simple and beautiful message. All Jesus really wants us to do is to love one another. It's so hard to do when I have so much mistrust and dislike for some people. Why is loving so hard?

Prayer

Dear God, give me a renewed heart big enough to love even the people I don't like to be near. Please help me to…

My Thoughts: Steve Jaeger

I think that it can be so hard to love others because either we were not properly loved ourselves, or we do not entirely understand what love is. People often misinterpret love. Some people even choose not to love at all. I know that I'm not sure what love is because its actions have not really been defined for me. Love is a feeling with long-term actions and effects. I never know what act is from love until years after it has happened.

❧•❧

Sixth Sunday of Easter (Cycle A)

Acts 8:5–8, 14–17

When the new work list was made up, Philip was assigned to preach in Samaria, which was about thirty miles away. A large crowd came up to hear him. He was a very convincing talker and afterward many people asked to become Christians. He baptized all who asked him. Then a few weeks later Peter and John were assigned to go to Samaria. The trip was made to confirm with the Holy Spirit all the people who had been baptized by Philip.

Psalm 66:1–3a, 4–7a, 16, 20 *Let's tell the whole world how great God is*

God is good to all of us. Let's give God thanks for everything. God has always been there to help us. God was there for our ancestors. I've never been disappointed when I've prayed to God.

1 Peter 3:15–18

St. Peter wrote a letter that said, Whenever you pray, you should thank Jesus for all that has been done for you. His whole reason for coming to earth and dying for us was so he might lead us to God. He came to show us how the children of God should live. Whatever you do in life, you should do a good job of it. It should be a good enough job that you would be proud to sign it: "Made by a child of God," or "Produced by a child of God," or "Packed by a child of God."

John 14:15–21

Jesus talked to his close friends one day. He said, "I'm very serious about this. If you love me, prove it by living good lives. In a short while I'm going to leave you and go back to God in heaven. However, I won't leave you without help. I'll send you the Holy Spirit, who will give you the strength and courage and wisdom to carry on the good work you are all doing now. Remember, if you really love me, you will live good lives. And if you live good lives, God will love you in return."

Further Reflection

Although Jesus relaxed and seemed to enjoy himself, his message was a serious one: love with all your heart. I'm not always that way. Sometimes I'm in a rotten mood, and loving people is the last thing I want to do. Maybe I should be more serious about living the message as Jesus insisted on us doing just that.

Prayer

Dear God, I know and believe I am a child of yours. Help me to always act that way. Please help me to…

My Thoughts: Gina Glow

I just keep asking and trying to love others as God does. I know it is not an easy thing to do but the more I do it, the easier it becomes. I get and feel so much joy when in some small or big way I can show them the love of Christ by my actions. I feel like God has called us all to love others in whatever way we know how. I feel he calls us not just to love those we know or who are familiar to us but to reach out and love strangers just the same. Loving a stranger could be as simple as saying, "Hi, how was your day?" or, "You look tired, can I help you carry that onto the bus?"

Sixth Sunday of Easter (Cycle B)

Acts 10:25–26, 34–35, 44–48

One afternoon Peter went to visit a guy who was going to become a Christian. His name was Cornelius. When Cornelius saw Peter, he acted as though Peter was some superstar. Peter said to him, "Stop acting so crazy. I'm just an ordinary person like you are." Cornelius snapped out of it and acted more normal after that. While Peter was there, he talked to some friends and relatives of Cornelius's too. He said, "Recently, I've noticed that God doesn't show any favorites. He doesn't like one race of people better than another. If any person acts in a good way, God is happy."

Almost as soon as Peter finished talking, all the people listening were filled with the Holy Spirit. Some of the people were Jews and some were not. Then Peter said, "Since you have all received the Holy Spirit, there's no reason why you shouldn't be baptized if you want to be." So they were all baptized and then they talked Peter into staying a couple of extra days to talk some more with them.

Psalm 98:1–4 *Sing a new song to God*

Let's make up a new song to sing to God because God's done so many wonderful things for us. We know that God has saved us. We know that God is just and holy and kind and faithful. God is willing to save everyone in the world. Everyone should sing for joy to God for God is good.

1 John 4:7–10

St. John wrote a letter that said, It's time we seriously started loving one another because God is love and anyone who loves is a child of God. If a person doesn't love, then that person has nothing to do with God. What's very important to remember is that God loved us so much that the Son was sent to show us how to live. That's why it's important that we love.

John 15:9–17

Jesus said to his friends one day, "The way God loves me is the same way I love you. I want you to always remember that I really love you all. All I want you to do in return is to love each other as I have loved you. If you do this, you will really be my closest friends. I want you to know something else, too. I learned it a long time ago. There is no greater love in the world than that of a person who is willing to give up his or her life for a friend. I don't ask much from you, but I do ask one favor from all of you: that you love one another."

Further Reflection

Jesus is right. He doesn't ask too much from us for all we've been given.

Prayer

Dear God, thank you for loving me and sending your Son to show me how to live. Help me to love others as I have been loved. Please help me to…

My Thoughts: Joe Curry

Please help me to show others that I care about them. Sometimes showing love for others means going out on a limb to extend kindness and words of appreciation. Love is something that cannot always be verbalized, so please help me to listen for the words unspoken.

❧❧•❧❧

Sixth Sunday of Easter (Cycle C)

Acts 15:1–2, 22–29

There was a big argument brewing among the different communities whether the men members had to be circumcised or not. Paul and Barnabas went to Peter and the other apostles to discuss the problem. The apostles decided to send reps with Paul and Barnabas to tell the people about their decision not to burden people with circumcision, if that wasn't part of their local customs. It was a relief to most of the men to hear that news.

Psalm 67:2–3, 5–6, 8 *God, we praise you for your goodness*

God, help us. Let your face shine on us and we will be saved. You have been good to all peoples. Everyone should bless your name.

Revelation 21:10–14, 22–23

St. John wrote, In a vision an angel took me to the top of a mountain. I could see all of Jerusalem from there. It was a beautiful city. Everything was in perfect order. There were twelve gates into the city and each was named for one of the twelve tribes. The Temple was truly something to see. God presided over it all.

John 14:23–29

Jesus said, "If you love me you will keep my words. Then God and I will come and dwell within you. I'm going to send the Paraclete shortly so you will be reminded of all that I taught you. So don't worry when I leave you. Be happy for me. I wish peace for all of you."

Further Reflection

Peace is what Jesus wanted to leave us with. It seems so funny when we look around and see even families torn apart. I guess if I want it to happen, it has to start with me.

Prayer

Dear God, sometimes I get so caught up in such petty things that I forget to look at the bigger picture. Instead of trying to make everything perfect here and now, I think I'll wait until heaven for that to happen. Please help me to...

My Thoughts: Jenny Tomes

Today I got so consumed by my desires to be perfect that I lost all focus on the bigger picture of what my life is for. I put aside what I love and value only to find myself empty and alone. Getting sucked into unrealistic standards cannot let me shine. With all the stress and chaos of my life, I cannot afford to push away the peace Jesus is continually offering me. Thankfully, when I lose myself and stumble, the gift of peace is still being given.

❧❧•❧❧

Seventh Sunday of Easter (Cycle A)

Acts 1:12–14

After Jesus had left them for good, his friends went back to their homes and started to pray for courage and strength. They prayed very hard that God would send them the Holy Spirit as Jesus had said he would.

Psalm 27:1, 4, 7–8a *All good things come from God*

God, you are the light that shows me the way to go. You have saved me. There is nothing I need fear. There is only one thing I really want. I want always to live a good life of helping other people. I want to do your will.

1 Peter 4:13–16

St. Peter wrote a letter that said, You should spend your life doing good for other people. You should love everyone and try to help everyone the best way you can. That is what Christ wants of you. Don't let anyone find anything bad to say about you. Don't become insensitive to other people. Don't go around killing or stealing or hurting others. Lead good lives!

John 17:1–11a

One night Jesus was alone. He spent the time thinking and praying to God. He said, "God, my work here on earth is almost over. Please give me the strength to stay at it till the end. I'd like to pray for my friends too. They are really very good people. Since I will be leaving them soon, they're going to need all the help you can give them."

Further Reflection

A lot of the Scriptures recently have been about praying. Sometimes I don't pray as often or as hard as I should.

Prayer

Dear God, you deserve all my attention and time. You've given me every-thing. I need to give you more of my time in prayer. Please help me to…

My Thoughts: David Klein

I disagree with the statement about not letting anyone find anything bad to say about you. I think that people should do what they think God wants them to do and not worry about what anybody thinks about you. People only want what's best for themselves, and they don't know your situation as well as you do, so trust yourself and don't worry about what others think.

爨•爨

Seventh Sunday of Easter (Cycle B)

Acts 1:15–17, 20–26

The apostles needed to replace Judas after he killed himself. They had an election. They picked two names and then after they prayed, they drew lots. Barsabbas and Matthias were the choices. Matthias was picked.

Psalm 103:1–2, 11–12, 19–20 *God is the greatest*

Bless God with all we have. God's been so good to us. No one is greater than our God.

1 John 4:11–16

St. John wrote a letter that said, As God loves us, so we must love others. God abides in us. God's love is in us. We have to share it.

John 17:11–19

Jesus looked up to heaven and prayed, "God, keep a good eye on my friends. They've really been doing a good job of spreading the word about your goodness. I'd hate to have anything happen to them. Take care of them and do with me what you want."

Further Reflection

It's hard to believe that there are people who really don't believe in God. It's hard to believe when *we* see what joy our faith brings to us.

Prayer

Dear God, thanks for giving me my faith in you. I couldn't do it without you. Please help me to...

My Thoughts: David Klein

I don't think it was right to hold an election to become a disciple. You should not have to be elected to be able to spread the word of God. If someone wants to give their life to spread the good news, they should be able to.

爨•爨

Seventh Sunday of Easter (Cycle C)

Acts 7:55–60

Stephen had a vision where he saw the Son of God standing at God's right hand. The people who were going to kill Stephen didn't want to hear anything he was saying so they shouted loudly and even covered their ears. When they started to stone him, he prayed that God would take his spirit and forgive his killers. Paul was in the crowd when this was happening, but he wasn't a believer at that point.

Psalm 97:1–2, 6–7, 9 *God is really our only ruler*

God is the true ruler of us all. God began everything and keeps it going. God, you are the greatest.

Revelation 22:12–14, 16–17, 20

St. John wrote, I heard a voice say, "Remember I'm coming soon. So everyone who is thirsty, let them come and receive the living waters."

John 17:20–26

Jesus prayed, "God, I place in your care not only my disciples but those who come to believe *through* my disciples. May they all be of one accord in us. May your love for me be in them and may I also live in them."

Further Reflection

What a beautiful prayer Jesus made on our behalf. He prayed that all generations, whoever came to know him, would live in peace and harmony with God for all time.

Prayer

Dear God, I want to be one with you. Take everything from me that would prevent that from happening. Take my sins and evil inclinations and replace them with love and kindness. Please help me to...

My Thoughts: Becky Musolf

I feel the prayer for this goes well with the passages. It is a lot easier saying you are a good person than it is to actually be one, so the prayer is very thoughtful and realistic. The passages also reassure me that God will always be with me helping to give me answers to life and the strength to go on in life.

My Thoughts: Kristin Nelson

These passages make me think of forgiveness. Both Stephen and Jesus were so concerned with their persecutors. I know this is an area where I need strength. A possible ending to this prayer could be "...forgive all who commit acts of unkindness toward me. Help me to remember they also are your children."

FOUR
END OF THE EASTER SEASON

Ascension of the Lord (Ascension Thursday) (Cycle A)

Acts 1:1–11

Just before he left the disciples and ascended into heaven, Jesus promised to send them the Holy Spirit. They were encouraged to keep the faith and spread it until Jesus came back at the final coming.

Psalm 47:2–3, 6–9 *Everyone, sing of God's goodness*

Clap your hands and shout for joy. God is the greatest. Sing joyful songs to God. Sing joyful songs about God. God is the greatest.

Ephesians 1:17–23

St. Paul wrote a letter that said, May God give you every blessing imaginable, may your faith be strong, and your hope enthusiastic. Belief in Christ means everything. Keep that faith alive until he comes again.

Matthew 28:16–20

The eleven went to the mountain where Jesus planned to meet with them. He told them, "Go out and make disciples of all peoples. Baptize in the name of the Father and of the Son and of the Holy Spirit. Teach them everything I told you to. And remember, I'll be with you always."

Further Reflection

Spread the good news. Live it in your life on a daily basis. That seems to be what Jesus wants all of us to do. And we can, with the help of the Spirit in our lives.

Prayer

Dear God, I want to please you in all things. Help me do that with the grace of your Spirit abiding in my life. Please help me to…

My Thoughts: Zach Czaia

In all of today's readings, there is an exhortation to us to tell others about the gift of faith we have been given. David says, "Sing to God, sing about God," and Christ encourages his apostles to "go out and make disciples of men." Christ's angels (heaven's angels) also said, "He will come

59

again in the same way he has left." We must make ready our souls for his return, so one day Christ will be fully in us and we fully in him. This preparation can be found in a daily prayer life and regular use of Christ's gifts, the sacraments.

❧❧•❧❧

Ascension of the Lord (Cycle B)

Acts 1:1–11

Just before he left the disciples and ascended into heaven, Jesus promised to send them the Holy Spirit. They were encouraged to keep the faith and spread it until Jesus came back at the final coming.

Psalm 47:2–3, 6–9 *Everyone, sing of God's goodness*

Clap your hands and shout for joy. God is the greatest. Sing joyful songs to God. Sing joyful songs about God. God is the greatest.

Ephesians 1:17–23

St. Paul wrote a letter that said, May God give you every blessing imaginable, may your faith be strong, and your hope enthusiastic. Belief in Christ means everything. Keep that faith alive until he comes again.

Mark 16:15–20

When the day finally came for Jesus to leave and go to his Father, he met with his friends and he said to them, "This is the last time I'll see you all face to face. It's time for me to go back to my Father. What I'm going to tell you now is very important. I want you to go out into the world and tell people about God's love for them. Baptize them in the name of the Father and of the Son and of the Holy Spirit. Teach them everything I have taught you. Anyone who believes what you say and is baptized will be saved. And remember, although you won't be able to see me, I'll be with you always!" Then Jesus was taken up to heaven to be with his Father forever. The friends of Jesus went out and did everything Jesus told them to do.

Further Reflection

Spread the good news. Live it in your life on a daily basis. That seems to be what Jesus wants all of us to do. And we can, with the help of the Spirit in our lives.

Prayer

Dear God, I want to please you in all things. Help me do that with the grace of your Spirit abiding in my life. Please help me to...

My Thoughts: Tom Klein

I think it is interesting how years ago people were baptized late in life but now we are baptized shortly after birth. Why and when did that change? I think it is done at birth now to forgive us of original sin, but what is the point of that? A six-month-old baby has no capability of committing sin.

❧❧•❧❧

Ascension of the Lord (Cycle C)

Acts 1:1–11

Just before he left the disciples and ascended into heaven, Jesus promised to send them the Holy Spirit. They were encouraged to keep the faith and spread it until Jesus came back at the final coming.

Psalm 47:2–3, 6–9 *Everyone, sing of God's goodness*

Clap your bands and shout for joy. God is the greatest. Sing joyful songs to God. Sing joyful songs about God. God is the greatest.

Ephesians 1:17–23

St. Paul wrote a letter that said, May God give you every blessing imaginable, may your faith be strong, and your hope enthusiastic. Belief in Christ means everything. Keep that faith alive until he comes again.

Luke 24:46–53

After Jesus gave the apostles a few last-minute instructions, he took them out of the city, blessed them for one last time, and then was taken up to heaven. They went back to the city and continued to do the preaching that he wanted them to do when he was gone.

Further Reflection

Spread the good news. Live it in your life on a daily basis. That seems to be what Jesus wants all of us to do. And we can, with the help of the Spirit in our lives.

Prayer

Dear God, I want to please you in all things. Help me do that with the grace of your Spirit abiding in my life. Please help me to...

My Thoughts: Will French

These readings all speak about faith and carrying on Jesus' works after he has gone. Faith is a very strange thing, a very rare thing, to put absolute and complete trust in someone or something is not easily done. I cannot think of anyone I would trust completely. I am not a pessimistic or suspicious person. I have many close friends and family members, but still the only person on this earth I have complete trust in—faith, if you will—is myself.

☙•❧

Pentecost Sunday

Acts 2:1–11

Everyone was gathered in one place. All of a sudden a huge wind came up and filled the room. Tongues of fire descended on all who were present. They became filled with the Holy Spirit. Later that day when they went to proclaim the good news to the people outside, there were a lot of foreigners in town. The weird thing was that the foreigners heard and understood what the apostles had to say in their mother tongue. Greeks heard the apostles talking in Greek. Romans heard Latin. There must have been people from twenty different countries. Everyone agreed it must have been the work of God.

Psalm 104:1, 24, 29–31, 34 *God, send your Spirit*
to renew us

Bless God with all our soul, with all we have. God, we see your loving hand in all creation. We cannot live without you. We rejoice and sing your praises everywhere and at all times.

1 Corinthians 12:3–7, 12–13

St. Paul wrote a letter that said, Everyone has different talents and abilities, but it is the same Spirit of God who gives them to each of us. We are like the parts of one big body. We all have things to do that help out the whole body. We are all one. There are no differences that can separate us, one from the other. The same Spirit of God abides in all of us. We truly are one in Christ.

Sequence

Come, Holy Spirit, come into our lives. Fill us with light that we may see the truth. Wash us that we may be cleansed of our sins. Warm our cold hearts that we may love all-inclusively. Shower us with your gifts of wisdom and patience and fortitude. Help us to live virtuously.

John 20:19–23

On the first evening of the week Jesus appeared to his disciples and said, "Peace be with you always. As God has sent me, so I send you." He breathed on them and said, "Be filled with the Holy Spirit. If you forgive sins, they are forgiven. If you don't, they aren't."

Further Reflection

God's Spirit had a powerful effect on the disciples. It's the same Spirit that God offers to abide in my life. I just have to be willing.

Prayer

Dear God, your Spirit did wonderful things to the disciples of Jesus. They were filled with courage and strength and wisdom. Give me those gifts, too, that I might better serve you in all that I do. Please help me to...

My Thoughts: Tom Klein

Although God created each one of us differently, we each were given gifts that enable us to benefit others. The key is to recognize these gifts within us and to have the wisdom and strength to know where and how to apply them.

PART II

WEEKDAYS OF LENT AND THE EASTER SEASON

FIVE
Weekdays of Lent

ASH WEDNESDAY AND THE DAYS FOLLOWING
Ash Wednesday

Joel 2:12–18

God said, "You need to change your ways and come back to me. Change your hearts, not just outward appearances. Call all the people together, even the priests. Do some penance. Fast from eating for a while. Then I will take pity on you."

Psalm 51:3–6, 12–14, 17 *God, be merciful for we have done wrong*

Have mercy on me, God. Take away my sins. Wash me from them all. I have done wrong. I admit it. Give me a clean heart. Give me the desire to do it your way.

2 Corinthians 5:20—6:2

St. Paul wrote a letter that said, I beg you in Christ's name to turn back to God's ways and stop sinning. Now's the time to clean up your act. There's no time like the present.

Matthew 6:1–6, 16–18.

Jesus said to his friends, "When you give to the poor, don't make a big show of it. When you are praying, don't do it in front of everyone so they'll think you're really holy. When you fast, don't make a big production of it. If you do everything for show, you'll already have the only reward you're going to get."

Further Reflection

This is the first day of Lent. I'm going to use this time in preparation for Easter to work on some things that I need to change in my life. I'm going to try to do it with all sincerity. I don't want to do it just for show so people will think I'm such a good person.

Prayer

Dear God, help me to become a better person. You've done so much for me. I know I can do better. Change me, mold me, shape me from the inside out. Please help me to…

My Thoughts: AR

It's sad to think how filled I am with attachments to things that don't really matter. I realize that I don't allow enough room for Jesus to enter my heart. I want to give up these attachments that hinder my relationship with God. This Lent I want to really open up my mind, body, and soul and let the love of the Lord fill me. I think it will help me to focus on all the sufferings and sacrifices Jesus made for me, and then the purging of my material attachments may seem easier.

❧❧●❧❧

Thursday after Ash Wednesday

Deuteronomy 30:15–20

Moses said to the people, "Today, I'm giving you a choice. You can follow God's ways and life, or you can follow other gods and surely perish. I hope you choose wisely because this decision will affect the generations to come after you."

Psalm 1:1–4, 6 *Happy are those who trust in God*

Happy are those who follow God's laws. Happy are those who try to do what is right. They will be blessed by God.

Luke 9:22–25

Jesus said, "The Son of God is going to have to suffer a lot and be put to death. But three days later he will be raised up. If you still want to follow me, you have to take up my cross and follow in my footsteps. If you lose your life for my sake, you'll actually save it. What good will it do you if you gain the wealth of the whole world and lose yourself in the process?"

Further Reflection

I have choices to make every day. Sometimes I don't want to make the right one. Sometimes it's easier just to go along with the crowd. Where would we be if that's what Jesus had done? I need to be more willing to go that extra mile that doing the right thing sometimes demands.

Prayer

Dear God, help me to do the right thing. Help me to follow in the steps of your Son. Please help me to…

My Thoughts: Tom Klein

I am reminded of the victim in the Columbine school shooting who was faced with the ultimate test of faith. With a gun pointed in her face, she was asked "Do you believe in God?" Answering "yes" cost the girl her life. I hope God grants me the strength to redeem myself through my faith during times that I am put to the test.

✼❀•❀✼

Friday after Ash Wednesday

Isaiah 58:1–9

God said, "Be straightforward in telling my people how it is. I want them to do the right things, but it is what is in their hearts that is really important. I'm not interested in the outward appearances but what's in their hearts. I'd rather they help one another, especially the poor and those in need, than to just fast and do penance. If they help those in need, then I will be willing to listen to them when they pray to me."

Psalm 51:3–6, 18–19 *God, be merciful to me*

Have mercy on me, O God. Take away my sins. Cleanse me real well. I admit I've done wrong. You're not interested in outward signs. You want a contrite heart.

Matthew 9:14–15

The elders of the people asked Jesus, "Why is it your followers don't fast? John the Baptist's do." Jesus responded, "They will, when the time is right."

Further Reflection

From outward appearances I seem like a really nice person. But sometimes if thoughts could kill, there would be no one alive around me. I really need to work on what's going on inside of me. Lent's a good time for that to happen.

Prayer

Dear God, be merciful to me and take away my evil ways, and especially my evil thoughts. They may not kill anyone, but they sure don't do anyone any good. Please help me to…

My Thoughts: David Klein

We have to tell people the truth about God's word. If we lie to them in order to get them to believe, people will soon discover the truth and become disillusioned with believing in him and his word. This is why straightforwardness is the best policy for spreading his message.

❧❧●❧❧

Saturday after Ash Wednesday

Isaiah 58:9–14

God said, "If you get rid of any oppression you see, if you stop lying, if you feed the hungry, then I will see to it that you want for nothing yourselves. I will renew you. Do what I ask and I will take care of you."

Psalm 86:1–6 *God, teach me your ways*

God, hear me when I pray to you. Protect me because I trust in you. Forgive me when I do wrong. Please listen to me. I'm begging you.

Luke 5:27–32

Jesus said to a tax collector, "Follow me." He did. His name was Levi. Later on Levi had Jesus over to his house for dinner. The elders of the people were shocked because tax collectors weren't the nicest of people to be hanging around with. They asked Jesus, "Why are you doing that? It's pretty revolting to us." Jesus answered back, "People who are healthy don't need to see a doctor. I have come to help those who need and really want to be helped."

Further Reflection

Sometimes I end up thinking that I'm so good. I start feeling pretty self-righteous. The fact is, there are a lot of things in my life that need to be changed.

Prayer

Dear God, keep me from thinking I'm so perfect. When I start to think that way I start pointing fingers at everyone else. I guess I really do that to throw the spotlight off me. Help me see what needs to be changed in my life, and help me have the courage to change some of it. Please help me to…

My Thoughts: Emily Miller

God will help you if you need it. He will take care of you if you ask. All he wants is for us to help others, if needed.

❧❧●❧❧

FIRST WEEK OF LENT
Monday, First Week of Lent

Leviticus 19:1–2, 11–18

God said to Moses, "Tell the people to start following *my* ways. I don't want them to be stealing or lying or cheating or swearing. I don't want them to do anything that will hurt another person. In fact, I want them to love their neighbor as themselves."

Psalm 19:8–10, 15 *God, your ways give us life*

God, your way is perfect. Your laws are the right way to live. Your command couldn't be clearer. God, your ways are true. You are our salvation.

Matthew 25:31–46

Jesus said, "When the Son of God comes in his glory, he will separate people into two groups: the good and the bad. He will say to the good, 'Come and be blessed for eternity, for when I was hungry and thirsty, you helped me. When I was in need, you visited me and sheltered me and clothed me. When you were nice and did these things for other people, you really did them for me." One could well imagine what the Son of God said to those who didn't live this way.

Further Reflection

It's very interesting what Jesus is saying today, because a lot of the time I just want to be left alone to vegetate. I don't want people around and I don't feel like doing anything for them, especially the people with whom I live. I may be in need of an attitude change.

Prayer

Dear God, sometimes I dream about saving the world and discovering the cure for all kinds of illnesses, but I'm not very good at making the people closest to me feel good about themselves. I want to live the way your Son taught us. Please help me to…

My Thoughts: Jason Merkel

Dear God, help me to love others, the way you have shown your love for me. Amen.

❧❦•❦❧

Tuesday, First Week of Lent

Isaiah 55:10–11

Just as the rain comes down and waters the plants and makes them grow abundantly, so shall God's word come down and cause people to grow in wisdom.

Psalm 34:4–7, 16–19 *God will help us*

Let us praise God for all the help we have received. When I prayed to God, my prayers were answered. God truly hears our prayers and helps us.

Matthew 6:7–15

Jesus said, "When you pray, make it simple. The truth is that God already knows what you're going to pray for. Here's how you might pray: 'God, you're the one and only. Your way, not mine. Your will, not mine. Please give me what I need sufficient for the day. Forgive me to the extent I forgive others. And please don't let the devil get hold of me. Amen.' "

Further Reflection

Sometimes I make everything so complicated, even my prayers. Jesus was to the point, and was up front in the things he did, even the way he taught us to pray.

Prayer

Dear God, life is so complicated and sometimes I make it even more complicated. More is not always better. Please help me to…

My Thoughts: David Klein

I think it is a very common misconception nowadays that we need to create long, elaborate prayers to reach God. If I were him, I wouldn't want to listen to long, boring prayers either. I prefer to just pray by holding a conversation with him, thanking him for all of the gifts in my life.

❦❧•❦❧

Wednesday, First Week of Lent

Jonah 3:1–10

God sent Jonah to a town called Nineveh to get them to change their bad ways. When he got there he said to the people, "If you don't clean up your act, this town is going to be destroyed in forty days." Believe it or not, the people actually listened and changed their lives. So the town was saved.

Psalm 51:3–4, 12–13, 18–19 *God loves those who have a change of heart*

Have mercy on me, God. Take my guilt from me and cleanse me of my sins. Renew my spirit. Keep me always in your sight. The best gift I can give God is a clean heart.

Luke 11:29–32

Jesus said, "This is an evil time. People are not living the way they should. People in the past changed their lives when the prophets warned them, but no one here will listen."

Further Reflection

The times haven't changed. The message hasn't changed. And I haven't changed all that much. The warning is there if I but heed it.

Prayer

Dear God, I want to do good, but there are so many distractions in my life. It doesn't seem to get easier, but rather harder to do what is right. Please help me to…

My Thoughts: Elizabeth R. Berning

We are living in evil times. Very few things are sure, but God's love is always a sure thing. If we ask him for mercy and work to be better people, we will be happy. God's love will save us. It's that simple.

❧•❧

Thursday, First Week of Lent

Esther 12:14–16, 23–25

Queen Esther prayed to God. She said, "God, please help me. I feel so alone. With your power save us. You can do all things."

Psalm 138:1–3, 7–8 *God answers our prayers*

I thank you, God, with all my heart. You have been kind and good. May your kindness endure forever.

Matthew 7:7–12

Jesus said, "Ask, and you will receive. Seek, and you will find. Knock, and it will be opened. God will answer your prayers, especially if you treat others the way you would like to be treated."

Further Reflection

A lot of the way God treats me seems to be hinged upon how I treat other people. There are some days when I probably just shouldn't pray to God if I'm not going to act nicer to the people around me.

Prayer

Dear God, I can be so petty and mean-spirited sometimes. Help me to act better. It's really unbecoming of me. Please help me to…

My Thoughts: Brian Melody

God will always listen to our prayers, but regrets that we don't treat others with respect. If we ask God for help, he must first show us the path to leading a friendlier life. It is through this path that we find the answer to our prayers.

❧❧•❧❧

Friday, First Week of Lent

Ezekiel 18:21–28

God said, "Turn from your evil ways and do good. If you are doing good now, don't change. The only way to really live your life is to do good."

Psalm 130:1–8 *Trust in God*

With all my heart I pray to you, God. Please listen to me. I beg you. I trust in you. I wait for your response. Your answer is always full of kindness and compassion.

Matthew 5:20–26

Jesus said, "You heard it said not to commit murder. I tell you not to get angry or abusive. If you start to bring your gift to the altar and realize you are harboring something against another person, leave your gift and first go be reconciled. Then you can come back and make your offering to God with a clean heart. Take care of this matter when it first occurs, or you'll pay for it later."

Further Reflection

There certainly are some people in my life whom I could treat a lot better than I do now. I shouldn't let all that anger boil up inside of me. I should take some positive action to work things out.

Prayer

Dear God, some people just drive me up the wall. There's no pleasing them. And there is no way they can be acceptable to my way of thinking. Maybe I ought to change my way to God's way. Please help me to…

My Thoughts: Annette Johnson

Help me to be willing to ask forgiveness. Help me to recognize my faults and say, "I'm sorry" to those whom they affect.

❧❧•❧❧

Saturday, First Week of Lent

Deuteronomy 26:16–19

Moses said to the people, "Follow God's ways with all your heart and soul. God is making a pact with us. We will be God's children and God will be our protector."

Psalm 119:1–2, 4–5, 7–8 *Happy are those who follow God's ways*

Happy are they who walk in God's ways. Happy are they who follow God's laws. Happy are they who have diligently kept them.

Matthew 5:43–48

Jesus said, "I tell you. You must love your enemies and even pray for them. This is really what God wants of you. What's so special about liking just people who like you back?"

Further Reflection

I don't have to look too far for people I don't like. Some of them are in my own immediate family. Some of them are at work. Some of them are at church, too. I've got some work to do if I really take this God stuff seriously.

Prayer

Dear God. I always thought I didn't have to like everyone. I just had to love everybody. I'm beginning to realize that's just a cop-out. I really do have to treat everyone the way I'd like to be treated. Please help me to…

My Thoughts: Michael Fenton

If we are to follow God's laws and live the way he wants us to live, then that entails we must follow and adhere to ALL of God's laws, which includes goodwill toward all people. Therefore, following just a single or a few of God's laws is just as bad as not following any. In the words of Abraham Lincoln, "Do you not destroy your enemies by making them your friends?"

My Thoughts: Amy

I've taken care of several people with mental disabilities. I find it funny that they can bite me, pinch me, pull my hair, hit me, say mean things, and I don't get offended or hold it against them. I don't take it personally and I still show them patience, care, and love. That is definitely a gift that I continually pray for as I work with them on correcting their behaviors. However, if a good friend of mine does the littlest thing to offend me, I take it personally, and sometimes I allow a grudge to fester. I need to pray for patience and acceptance of my close friends and family too. Prayer is a wonderful gift.

❧❧•❧❧

SECOND WEEK OF LENT
Monday, Second Week of Lent

Daniel 9:4–10

God, you have always been faithful to the covenant you made with us, but we haven't been as faithful on our part. We've done lots of things that are wrong. We're sorry. Please forgive us. We really want to do what is right.

Psalm 79:8–9, 11, 13 *God, be gentle with us*

God, please be compassionate with us. Help us. Forgive our sins. Then we can give you the praise you deserve.

Luke 6:36–38

Jesus said, "Be kind, as God is. Don't be judgmental, and you won't be judged. Forgive, and you'll be forgiven. Give, and you shall receive. The way you act toward others is the way they will treat you."

Further Reflection

Change. Do good. In fact, be generous. It's the way to go if we are to be happy in this life that is given to us. Why does it sound so simple, and yet is so hard to live? Maybe I haven't done the first thing that is necessary: change my heart.

Prayer

Dear God, take those things that keep me from doing your will, your way willingly. There are so many things that I should change in my life. Please help me to…

My Thoughts: Kristin Nelson

This makes me think about temptation. What we are supposed to do may seem so simple, but Satan is always lurking trying to tempt us by offering us something that may seem nice short-term, but hurts our long-term relationship with God. Jesus ultimately lays it out for us with the "Golden Rule," yet we consistently do what is displeasing to God to make ourselves "happy" only briefly. We all truly need a change of heart.

🐾●🐾

Tuesday, Second Week of Lent

Isaiah 1:10, 16–20

Listen to what God has to say: "Clean up your act. Stop doing all those evil things, and learn to do good. Work for justice for all. If you do good, more good will happen."

Psalm 50:8–9, 16–17, 21, 23 *Let us pray for God's saving power*

Don't just talk a good talk, walk it, too.

Matthew 23:1–12

Jesus said to the people, "Do what the leaders tell you to do, but don't necessarily act the way they do. A lot of them are self-serving. A lot of them wouldn't lift a finger to help someone in need. If you want to be great, be of service to those around you."

Further Reflection

Sometimes I get so shocked when I see how some people go so little out of their way to help people in need. There are many causes that I espouse because they're good for the environment and for all the creatures that walk on the earth. But sometimes that's all I do—talk. I need to act on some of my convictions rather than just point the finger at other people who should be doing something too.

Prayer

Dear God, there are so many things that need to be done to help make the world a better place to live and to build up your realm on earth. Sometimes there are so many choices that I don't know where to start. Please help me to...

My Thoughts: Angela Becker

Know that I can make a difference. Even though the way things are today can be discouraging, we still need the persistence to keep trying to spread your word. Please help me to continue spreading your word to those who are searching for the truth.

❧•❧

Wednesday, Second Week of Lent

Jeremiah 18:18–20

The people wanted to kill Jeremiah because he told it like it was. Jeremiah prayed real hard for God to help him.

Psalm 31:5–6, 14–16 *God, help me*

God, I put all my trust in you. Help me. People who don't believe in what I stand for want to kill me. I put my life in your hands. Please help me get through that.

Matthew 20:17–28

As they were going up to Jerusalem, Jesus warned his friends that things weren't going so well. He even indicated that he probably would be killed. The mother of James and John was always looking out for their good. She asked Jesus if, when he got to his kingdom, would he make sure that her two sons would get good seats next to him. Jesus said to her, "You don't really know what you are asking. Can they go through what I am going to go through?" The two disciples responded, "Sure we can." "Well, you will, but as for those good seats, God is the one who says where people will end up." When the other apostles heard about all this vying for special places of honor, they got mad. Jesus said, "If you want to be the greatest and be honored, then serve those around you now."

Further Reflection

Jesus is very insistent about helping the people around us. He spent his entire life doing just that. Money, prestige, power—none of them seem as important to Jesus as being kind and helpful to other people. It should be my priority too.

Prayer

Dear God, I want to be liked and have people think I'm someone special. Your son seems to think I will be like that if I try to help other people. Please help me to...

My Thoughts: Chris Keyser

Nothing worthwhile is easy to get these days. We all want something in our lives and it usually isn't handed to us. We have to earn it. Just as we earn respect or prestige or material goods, we must also earn the respect of God by doing good deeds for others.

❧❧•❧❧

Thursday, Second Week of Lent

Jeremiah 17:5–10

God said, "Trust in my ways, not in the evil ways of some humans. Just remember that in the end it will be me who rewards people according to the way they lead their lives."

Psalm 1:1–4, 6 *Happy are they who trust in God's ways*

Happy are they who follow God's laws. Happy are they who spend time praying to God for guidance. God watches over those who try to act justly.

Luke 16:19–31

Jesus said to the leaders of the people, "Once there was a rich person who ate great meals everyday. Outside the palace was a poor sick person who had almost nothing to eat and would have been more than grateful to eat the scraps from the rich person's table. At last they both died. The poor person went to Abraham's bosom. The rich, selfish person went to the place of punishment. The rich person called out asking for a sip of water, but Abraham said, "No can do. You're both getting what you deserve.

Anyway, there's no way we can get to you from where we are." The rich person said, "Well, maybe there's nothing you can do for me, but could you go back to earth and warn my siblings what will happen to them if they don't act better than they are." Abraham replied, "If they won't listen to people like Moses and the prophets, they won't listen to someone who would come back from the dead."

Further Reflection

How many times have I said, "If I had only known… If I could just do it over again." The fact is that I do know and I should be acting better. I don't need some sign from out of the blue to know how I should be living my life.

Prayer

Dear God, I really know what I should be doing. Give me the grace to do it. Please help me to…

My Thoughts: AR

Some days I think of all the wrong my friends do and think, Oh, they've done worse things than me so I should be okay to go to heaven. The gospel reminds me that maybe I should focus more on what I don't do, like how I don't always share my gifts with those who need them. Sometimes I do something nice and then I'll refuse to do something I should and think the first nice act was good enough. I really need to sacrifice and repent and pray more instead of thinking that I'm for sure going to heaven.

❧❧•❧❧

Friday, Second Week of Lent

Genesis 37:3–4, 12–13, 17–28

Israel really loved his youngest son the best. His siblings were extremely jealous of him and actually plotted to do away with him. While they were out working in the pasture, they threw him into a dry cistern where he would die of hunger and thirst. After they did their dastardly deed, they sat down and started to eat together. While they were finishing their meal, a caravan going to Egypt went by. They got an idea to sell their brother into slavery and make some money off him instead of just letting him die. They got twenty pieces of silver that they divided equally among them.

Psalm 105:16–21 *Remember the good things God has done for us*

When famine came upon the land, Joseph was in Egypt ready to help. Even though he was sold as a slave, he would help his siblings. The rulers of Egypt saw his great potential and gave him a position of power.

Matthew 21:33–43, 45–46

Jesus told the leaders of the people this story: "Once there was a person who planted a vineyard and then leased it out to tenants. When it was time for the harvest, he sent his servants to get his share of the crop. The tenants beat the servants up and wouldn't give the owner what was his due. Then he figured if he sent his son, they would respect the agreement that they had made. But they killed the son. Now what do you think the owner did to the tenants?" They responded, "We're sure he made them pay for his son's death." Jesus responded, "You know, in the long run, we're all going to pay for our actions."

Further Reflection

People sure can be mean to one another. There are a lot of cutthroats out there. People claim that when you point the finger at someone, there are three fingers pointing back. There are some things I could change in my life.

Prayer

Dear God, I could be a lot nicer to my siblings. Please help me to...

My Thoughts: Elizabeth R. Berning

When I was younger my siblings and I fought all the time. We would fight physically and verbally and cause my parents all sorts of headaches. As I've gotten older, our situation has improved and we are friends now. I still see other people fighting, though, whether it be with their siblings, parents, spouses, friends, coworkers, or employers. People are very selfish and forget the golden rule. It is only with prayer and patience that people can rise above this and be nice rather than mean.

❧❧●❧❧

Saturday, Second Week of Lent

Micah 7:14–15, 18–20

God, you treat your people with great kindness. They feel your comfort and care. God, there is no one like you. You forgive sins and wipe away any guilt. You are compassionate and faithful, and you fill us with grace.

Psalm 103:1–4, 9–12 *God is kind and merciful*

Bless God. Bless God's holy name. God forgives us our sins. God redeems our life. God is kinder than we deserve.

Luke 15:1–3, 11–32

One day Jesus told a story about how happy God is when a sinner stops sinning and returns to doing good. He said, "Once there was a man who had two sons. The younger one said, 'Give me right now the money that you would give me when you die. I want to get as far away from here as I can.' The father did. The son left and wasn't heard from for a long time. He squandered all that he had received from his father. At that time there was a terrible famine in the country. No one lifted a finger to help him, so he got a job on a farm taking care of pigs. He wasn't given much to live on and wanted to eat the food he fed the pigs, but it was against regulations. Pretty soon he didn't have a cent to his name. He really was starving when he began to think about his own country. He thought to himself, 'My father's workers have plenty to eat. I'll go back home and beg my father to let me be one of his hired hands.'

"So he set out toward home. When he was still far off, his father saw him coming. Beside himself with joy he ran to meet his son, threw his arms around him, kissed him, and wouldn't let him go. The son said, 'I've done so many things wrong. I don't deserve to be your son. Let me work for you as a hired hand.' The father would hear nothing of it. He had his servants clean him up and then they had a great welcome home party for him.

"The older brother was out in the field when all this was happening, and he got real mad when he heard what his father had done. He came in screaming, 'You've never done anything special for me or my friends. I've always been loyal to you. I worked hard all these years while he was out throwing all your money away. It's just not fair.'

"The father said, 'Look, son. I've always had you with me. Everything I have is yours. I just had to celebrate since your brother is home with us. I was sure he was dead by now. He's really alive and has come back to us. This really makes me happy. I hope you can understand that.' "

Further Reflection

I get jealous when I see something nice happen to other people, especially when I don't think they deserve it. But then, who am I to be judging other people?

Prayer

Dear God, thank you for the many blessings you have given me in my lifetime. Let me see your goodness wherever I look. Please help me to...

My Thoughts: Joe Curry

Use and explore my talents. Give me guidance in my musical journey that I may refine my talent to honor you during Mass and elsewhere. Help me appreciate and recognize without jealousy the gifts and blessings that you have bestowed on others.

THIRD WEEK OF LENT
Monday, Third Week of Lent

2 Kings 5:1–15

Naaman, a great army commander, had leprosy. One of his wife's servants told her about a powerful prophet who lived in Samaria who could cure her husband. The ruler of the land wrote a letter of introduction and sent the army officer to find the prophet. When he arrived, the ruler of Israel was put out that a leper from another country was sent to him. But the prophet was more welcoming and told Naaman he would be cured if he washed seven times in the Jordan River. The army commander was a little put out because he figured he could have just as easily washed in some river in his own country. He was expecting some kind of instant miracle. His servants said to him, "If the prophet had told you to stand on your head and you'd be cured, you would have done it. Why don't you try what he suggested?" He did and he was cured. From then on he believed in the God of Israel.

Psalm 42:2–3; 43:3–4 *I long to live with God*

As a deer in the forest longs for water, so I long to be with God. How long will it be before I see God face to face? God, send a light to guide me to your holy mountain. I want to stand before God's high altar and play forever on my harp.

Luke 4:24–30

Jesus said, "No prophets gain acceptance in their home town." The people didn't want to hear that kind of talk from Jesus. After all, a lot of them grew up with him. They were so mad they decided to throw him off a cliff, but he slipped through their hands and got away.

Further Reflection

It is kind of interesting. I'm a little like that commander in the first reading. I want some special signs from God so I can know that what I'm doing is right. I have to learn to see God's presence in the ordinary events of each day because our faith tells us God is always with us.

Prayer

Dear God, sometimes I get so caught up in the miracles and angels and stuff like that I forget you are here in the sunset, you are here in the smile of another person. Please help me to…

My Thoughts: Nicole Borchardt

God, I hope to see you in people I meet everyday and the things I do, no matter how small or unimportant they seem. Yes, Lord, I desire a great sign, but that is yours to give if and when you want. What is mine to do is to nurture my faith and grow in the midst of ordinary life, or rather *through* ordinary life. Thank you for each boring, uneventful day, because it is the chance to believe in what I do not see and to live for what I have not experienced, so that when you do decide to show me heaven, I will be found ready.

🎕❧●❧🎕

Tuesday, Third Week of Lent

Daniel 3:25, 34–43

Azariah stood up in the fire and prayed, "God, we will always keep our covenant with you. No matter what is done to us, we still stand steadfast. They can kill us but they can't take our faith from us."

Psalm 25:4–9 *God, don't forget us*

God, teach me your ways. Guide me to the truth. Be kind and compassionate.

Matthew 18:21–35

Peter asked Jesus, "When someone does something wrong to me, how many times must I forgive that person? Seven times?" "No," Jesus said, "You need to do it till it takes. I'd say seventy times seven, if need be. If you don't forgive, you yourself won't be forgiven."

Further Reflection

I love to hold grudges. They make me feel more important than the other person. They make me feel like I'm the victim. They bring out the worst in me.

Prayer

Dear God, help me to hand it all over to you. Help me to let go of all the past hurts. Help me to live in the present. Please help me to…

My Thoughts: Annette Johnson

Help to live in constant forgiveness, to let go of past wrongdoings—mine and others—in order to live fully in the company of God in the present. If there is a grudge there is no room for God. Help me to release the grudges and cling only to love.

❧•☙

Wednesday, Third Week of Lent

Deuteronomy 4:1, 5–9

Moses said to the people, "Now that we are going to enter the Promised Land, I want you to follow all the laws God has asked us to live by. Don't forget anything that I've handed on to you. Be sure to teach them to your children and their children."

Psalm 147:12–13, 15–16, 19–20 *Everyone, praise God*

Let us thank God. Everything we have comes from God. Even God's laws are wonderful and easy to follow.

Matthew 5:17–19

Jesus said to his friends, "Don't think that I have come to get rid of the law. I've come to make sure it is followed down to the very last one. It leads us straight to God."

Further Reflection

I hate rules. I hate people telling me what to do. Why can't we just do whatever we feel like doing? The simplest answer is that rules get us to where we're going the fastest and easiest way.

Prayer

Dear God, I don't like rules, but I also don't want to lose your presence in my life. Please help me to…

My Thoughts: Kortney Jendro

Like religion to faith
There lies a difference
'Tween our rules and our laws

There is the golden rule.
The rule of thumb
And playing by the
Rules of the game.

Then we have
Laws of nature
Murphy's Law
Cole's Law

Which do we honor more?
Are laws a byproduct of government only?
Do we give to Caesar what Caesar is due?

Or do we even have
Due process of law?
Can you see the difference 'tween
Statutes and commandments?
Rules and laws?

❧❀❧

Thursday, Third Week of Lent

Jeremiah 7:23–28

God said to the people, "Listen to my voice and heed what you hear." But they wouldn't listen and they wouldn't heed.

Psalm 95:1–2, 6–9 *If today you hear God's voice in your heart, follow it*

Come, everyone, let's sing to God. Let's tell the world that God has saved us. Let's thank God from the bottom of our hearts. Let's sing songs of praise to God. Come, let's bow our heads down and pray to God. In fact, let's kneel before God who made us. Don't grumble or argue like the people in the desert did when everything didn't go the way they expected it to.

Luke 11:14–23

While Jesus was casting out a devil, the people started to say that he got his power from the Devil himself. Jesus responded, "Why on earth would I be expelling devils if I get my power from the Devil himself? You don't make any sense."

Further Reflection

You can lead a horse to water but…Why do people have to do it their way? Why do people become so pigheaded that they just won't listen to the truth when it is presented to them? Why do I think I'm any different?

Prayer

Dear God, change my hardened heart. Please help me to…

My Thoughts: Becky Musolf

I really like this psalm. I often feel that I cannot hear what God is trying to tell me, or where I should be going in life. Sometimes I even feel he has let me down. This meditation helps me see that I need to listen harder and everything will work out in the end. I just need to be patient.

❦•❦

Friday, Third Week of Lent

Hosea 14:2–10

Turn back to God and be healed. God will love you freely. You shall blossom. The wise understand this. The prudent know this is the way to go.

Psalm 81:6–11, 14, 17 *Follow God's way*

God, when I was in distress, I called and you helped me. You are the God who has always helped us. We will put no other gods before you. You're our one and only.

Mark 12:28–34

One of the leaders asked Jesus, "What's the first and most important commandment?" Jesus answered, "Love God with every fiber of your being, heart, soul, mind, and strength. The second one is pretty important, too. Love your neighbor as yourself." "That's a great answer. Following them is greater than all the sacrifices we could make to God," the leader said.

Further Reflection

Put God first and treat our neighbors with respect are two things that make a lot of sense to me. God's given us everything we are and have. It's important to give God due respect. And since we are all made in God's image and likeness, since we're all God's children, we're equals, so we should treat each one with respect too.

Prayer

Dear God, you're number one in my book. If I'm to follow your way, every human is number two, including me. Please help me to…

My Thoughts: Steve Jaeger

I like how straightforward the message is: "God should be our primary focus." God has never turned us away nor let us down. This is the basis of our faith, right here. It's the basis of many different faith and is well put: "Greater than any sacrifice."

❦•❦

Saturday, Third Week of Lent

Hosea 6:1–6

When people are in pain, they will turn back to God, looking for help. It is God who has always been our help. We need to learn God's ways. It is love and respect that God is really looking for, not sacrifices.

Psalm 51:3–4, 18–21 *God wants our love and respect*

Have mercy on us, God. Take away our guilt. You're more interested in a humble heart than lots of sacrifices.

Luke 18:9–14

Jesus told this story one day, "Two people went up to the Temple to pray. One went right up front and said, 'Thank you, God, for making me who I am. I'm not like all those other people who lie and cheat and do all sorts of bad things. I'm really proud of all the good things I do.' The other one stayed toward the back and prayed, 'God, I'm a sinner. Please help me to be better.' Believe me, one went home feeling God's grace. The other didn't. Those who think they're so great, really aren't."

Further Reflection

Sometimes I think I'm pretty good. Sometimes I think I'm even better than most people. Jesus may have been talking about me. I should be a little more humble. After all, everything I have and am really comes from God in the first place.

Prayer

Dear God, when I get to thinking I'm better than most people, knock me down a peg or two. Please help me to…

My Thoughts: AR

Some days I experience moments that humble me. Then I start thinking that finally, I'm a humble person! However, the moment someone says something negative about me, offends me, or accuses me wrongly of something, I get angry and defensive. I forget to be humble, forget to forgive, and focus on making myself look good. Living a humble life is tough! I think we should all pray for each other to become humble.

❧☙•❧☙

FOURTH WEEK OF LENT
Monday, Fourth Week of Lent

Isaiah 65:17–21

God said, "I am about to create a new world. The past will be forgotten. There will be no more tears or sorrow. Everyone will be happy and full of joy. People will live long and prosperous lives. They will own their own homes and eat from gardens they plant themselves."

Psalm 30:2, 4–6, 11–13 *God, thank you for saving me*

God, I am so glad you are always near me. I praise you for your goodness. You have always been my help. Thanks for everything.

John 4:43–54

While Jesus was in Capernaum, a royal official came to him with a request: "My child is almost dead. Help me!" Jesus responded, "Your child will live. Go home now." Later it was reported to the official that at that very moment Jesus was speaking to him, the child got better. The official became a lifelong believer in Jesus.

Further Reflection

I wish God would create a big miracle like that when I pray. I guess if my faith were stronger I would see that thousands of miracles have already happened in my life.

Prayer

Dear God, sometimes I can be so ungrateful. Sometimes I can miss all the beautiful "miracles" you shower me with every day of my life. Please help me to...

My Thoughts: Elizabeth R. Berning

Everyday is so beautiful. One of the ways I strive to see the miracles in my life is by thanking God each morning when I wake up. Every day is a miracle, even if it is not always easy to see. Some days I feel as though there is no good in my life and everything is really bad. I guess it's then that I should try to remember that there are miracles everywhere, if only I stop to see them.

❧ • ❧

Tuesday, Fourth Week of Lent

Ezekiel 47:1–9, 12

Ezekiel once had a vision of an eternal stream flowing out from the Temple that grew bigger and bigger the farther it flowed from the Temple. The land was full of wonderful vegetation and plant life. There were all kinds of wild animals feeding on the land. People not only used the plants for their food but also for medicine.

Psalm 46:2–3, 5–6, 8–9 *God is always with us*

God is our help and our strength. There is nothing we should fear. God is with us morning, noon, and night. How wonderful God is to us.

John 5:1–3, 5–6

While Jesus was in Jerusalem to celebrate one of the holy days, he stopped by the famous fountain of Bethesda. The waters of the fountain were known to heal people. There was a sick person by the water who had been ill for thirty-eight years and was hoping to be healed. Jesus knew some of his story so he said to the man, "Stand up. You're cured." He got up and sure enough, he was completely cured. The leaders of the people, who were already jealous of Jesus, decided to use the fact that Jesus cured this man on the Sabbath against him.

Further Reflection

They say Scriptures speak directly to us. I don't like all that I hear when I listen. Sometimes I feel like the leaders of the people in this story. If I don't like certain people, I try to turn around even the good that they do and use it against them.

Prayer

Dear God, open my eyes that I might see the truth. Open my ears that I might hear your truth. Open my heart that I might change some of my attitudes. Please help me to...

My Thoughts: Annette Johnson

Help me to not be such a hypocrite when it comes to people that I don't like. Help me to stop having such a selfish view of my beliefs. Help me to open myself to learning from others.

❧❀❧

Wednesday, Fourth Week of Lent

Isaiah 49:8–15

There will come a time when God will make all things new. People will want for nothing. God will be with them and never forget them.

Psalm 145:8–9, 13–14, 17–18 *God is kind and merciful*

God is good toward all. God is always faithful. God is always there to help us.

John 5:17–30

Jesus said, "Everything I have comes from God. If you follow my way, you'll live."

Further Reflection

God is always there to help us. It's a simple truth that makes sense. I need to rely on God more and stop thinking I have to do everything by myself.

Prayer

Dear God, direct me in your ways today. Please help me to...

My Thoughts: Jenny Tomes

I get so caught up with control. And when I'm not thinking "total control," I'm busy wondering what God wants me to do to better further his plan...make it better. Either way it's become a focus of my role, not God's. If she's always there (that makes sense), why did I feel a need to make the choices? God is far wiser, knows what's best, but I got sidetracked and think the opposite.

✦

Thursday, Fourth Week of Lent

Exodus 32:7–14

God said to Moses, "Go talk to the people. I'm very disappointed in them. They're worshiping a golden cow that they made while you were up on the mountain talking to me. I'm ready to get rid of all of them." Moses said, "Let me talk to them and see if they will repent and change their ways before you punish them all. After all, you did make a promise to their ancestor Abraham to make them as numerous as the stars in the sky." Moses made a good point, so God didn't kill them all right then and there.

Psalm 106:19–23 *God, remember us lovingly*

Our ancestors forgot the true God and worshiped a golden cow. They forgot about the God who freed them and brought them to the Promised Land. When God wanted to get rid of them, Moses came to their defense.

John 5:31–47

Jesus said, "Look at the things I do. They speak for me. It's obvious that I come from God for the things I do are of a loving nature. I come in God's name and yet your hearts are closed to all I do."

Further Reflection

Both of these readings speak to where I am sometimes. There are times when I put things and my own selfish pleasures before God. I'm sure glad that the God we worship is a loving and forgiving God.

Prayer

Dear God—cars, money, prestige, fame, fortune, travel...sometimes these are the things I put first in my life. Where are my priorities? Please help me to...

My Thoughts: AR

The words of God to the chosen people went unheeded. They succumbed to a sort of realistic despair ("Moses and his God have led us into a desert to die; why not enjoy our last moments here?") And so they constructed a new god and celebrated his arrival with acts of sin. It was their lack of trust that angered God. He was not angered that they could not see the moral good of their wandering through the desert (because if we put ourselves in their shoes, we would find it pretty tough to suffer joyfully, too). This was the God who had delivered them from evil, a God who asked only that they would obey and trust him. But they were blinded by reality and so succumbed to a very real cynicism in the golden calf. In a like manner, the scribes of Christ's time were so enmeshed in the political and polemical battles of their time period (struggles with Rome and struggles for power with each other), they were blind to the bright light of Christ's truths. In my life, I pray for a vivid moral imagination, so I can see beyond the drudgery of the everyday and catch at least a glimpse of God's purpose for me in the great scheme. Let me "think big" for God.

❦❦•❦❦

Friday, Fourth Week of Lent

Wisdom 2:1, 12–22

Some wicked people said, "Let's kill this guy. He thinks he's a child of God. He does all the right stuff. He makes us look bad. If he's really from God, God will save him." They were heartless people.

Psalm 34:17–21, 23 *God is near*

When the just cry out, God listens. God saves them from harm. God is close. God saves those in trouble.

John 7:1–2, 10, 25–30

Jesus went up to Jerusalem for the feast of the booths. He tried to do it quietly because by this time there were a lot of the leaders who wanted to have him killed. Some people recognized him in the crowd and started asking, "Isn't this the one the leaders want to kill if they find him because he claims he's the Messiah?" Jesus answered, "So you recognize me? The truth is that I come from God. God's sent me to do this work." They were horrified at what he was saying so they tried to grab him and kill him themselves. But he got away.

Further Reflection

Sometimes I don't live my life the way God and Jesus would like me to. In a sense, not living his way might be almost as bad as those people in the gospel who wanted to kill him outright.

Prayer

Dear God, I can be such a jerk sometimes. The whole reason you created me was so I could love you in return. And sometimes I just don't feel like doing it. Please help me to…

My Thoughts: Tom Klein

Everything in the Scriptures has a meaning and a purpose. The purpose of Jesus escaping the group was so that he could later be killed on the cross and rise on the third day in order to fulfill the Scriptures. The only part I don't understand is why sometimes he escaped angry mobs and at the end of his life he didn't? I understand God had a plan, but this mob could have been the one that was supposed to kill Jesus.

❧•❧

Saturday, Fourth Week of Lent

Jeremiah 11:18–20

Jeremiah said he knew they were out to get him, but he went willingly anyway. Someday, they'll get what they deserve.

Psalm 7:2–3, 9–12 *God, in you I take shelter*

God, you are my refuge. Protect me from those who would do harm to me. I've tried to do what is right. You know what is going on because you search the souls and hearts of all.

John 7:40–53

Some people thought Jesus was the Messiah. Others didn't. Some even plotted to have him arrested. When the leaders of the people thought they finally had enough on him, they were disappointed because the people who were going to arrest him chickened out.

Further Reflection

I can't believe the hatred some people had for Jesus. They were so angry with him they wanted to kill him. How unjust they were. There are times when I hate people around me. Why can I see how wrong it was for people to hate Jesus, but it's all right for me to hate some people?

Prayer

Dear God, sometimes I can see the faults of others so clearly. Help me to see the errors of my own foolishness and do something about it. Please help me to…

My Thoughts: Will French

What this says to me is how it is always easier for an outside observer to make judgments than someone involved in the situation. If someone accidentally hurts another person, it is much easier for someone else to realize it was an accident then it is for the person who is hurt. When you are involved in something sometimes you need to take a step back, calm down, and think about what you are doing.

❧ ● ❧

FIFTH WEEK OF LENT
Monday, Fifth Week of Lent

Daniel 13:1–9, 15–17, 19–30, 33–62

There were two dirty old men who wanted a woman named Susanna to sleep with them. When she rightly refused they told her they would make up a lie about her having sex with a young man and take her to court on the trumped-up charges. The penalty for that was death, but she refused to give in to them. They falsely had her charged and when they went to court, each gave his version of what happened. The judge decided to ask the two old men some questions individually to see if their stories matched. When they didn't agree, the judge knew they were lying and so freed Susanna. The two old men were put to death for what they tried to do to Susanna.

Psalm 23:1–6 *God, you are with me*

God is my provider. There is nothing I shall want. I have everything I need to refresh my body and soul. I fear no evil for God is at my side. God has anointed me with the oil of gladness. My cup overflows. Only goodness and kindness follow me all the days of my life. I know I shall eventually dwell in God's house.

John 8:1–11

A woman was caught committing the act of adultery. Jesus said to the people, "Let the one without sin cast the first stone." Everyone left because no one was without sin. Jesus told the woman not to do that sin again.

John 8:12–20 (Cycle C)

Jesus said to the people, "I am the light of the world. No one who follows me will ever be in darkness." This was all too much for some of them. They thought Jesus was talking off the top of his head.

Further Reflection

Why would people like those two men in the first reading make up a story about someone else? Why wouldn't some of the people believe what Jesus had to say? I'd like to think that I don't make up stories and that I follow everything that Jesus suggests we do, but I know I've made up stories to make myself look better than I am. I know I haven't always followed what Jesus wants of me.

Prayer

Dear God, let me know your will and let me have the guts to do it. Please help me to...

My Thoughts: David Klein

The story about Susanna is proof that doing the right thing will allow you to be saved by Jesus. She did the right thing by not sleeping with the men, and in the end, the lady was shown to be just and she was saved. Many times God works in roundabout ways, but he is always there.

❧•❧

Tuesday, Fifth Week of Lent

Numbers 21:4–9

The people started to grumble to Moses, "Why did you ever lead us out here into the desert? We were better off back in our slavery. There's nothing to eat here. We're just going to die out here." As a punishment for their disbelief, snakes were sent to bite and kill them. Finally, following God's instructions, Moses made a bronze snake and put it on a pole and walked among the dying people. Those that looked upon God's snake lived.

Psalm 102:2–3, 16–21 *God, please listen to my prayers*

God, lend an ear to my pleas. When I call out, please listen. All the nations revere your name. You help those in desperate need. We'll teach the next generation all about you.

John 8:21–30

Jesus said to the leaders of the people, "I am from above. You are from down below. You must change and believe in who I am. God sent me. I do nothing by myself." Some actually came to believe in him because he spoke so convincingly.

Further Reflection

Sometimes I wish I were in another place than where I am. Things seem greener elsewhere. My sense, though, is that God wants us to deal with the reality that we live in and not always be daydreaming about some better place that, in fact, doesn't exist.

Prayer

Dear God, help me to see your goodness in where I am in life, rather than trying to live in a fantasy world. Please help me to...

My Thoughts: David Klein

I think God wants us to daydream and fantasize about better places than where we are, especially heaven. That would serve to hold reverence for the kingdom that Jesus opened up for us with his death. It also makes us work to improve the world around us to reach that better place.

※⬦⬦⬦

Wednesday, Fifth Week of Lent

Daniel 3:14–20, 91–92, 95

The king said to the three brothers, "If you don't worship the golden statue I have ordered everyone to worship, I'll throw you into a furnace while you're still alive." The brothers said, "You might as well go ahead with your plan right now, because we're not going to worship your god." The king was madder than he'd ever been. He ordered the furnace to be heated to seven times normal. They were thrown in but then the king saw a fourth figure in the flames walking around with the brothers. "It must be an angel sent by their God to help them," the king said in disbelief.

(Psalm) Daniel 3:52–56 *Praised be God forever*

Blessed are you, God of our ancestors. Blessed is your holy name. Blessed are you in your temple. Blessed are you on your throne. Blessed are you everywhere and forever.

John 8:31–42

Jesus said, "If you live according to my teaching, you will really be one of my disciples. You will know the truth and the truth will set you free." "We aren't slaves. What do you mean we'll be set free?" some of the people asked. Jesus responded, "If you sin, you're a slave to that way of life. You have a closed mind toward me. No matter what I say, you'll twist it around and try to use it against me. You'll never believe that it is God who sent me."

Further Reflection

The king tried to kill the three brothers because they thought and worshiped differently than he did. The people finally killed Jesus basically because he thought differently than they did. There has been a lot of killing all done in the name of religion down through the centuries. There still is. In my heart there have been people in my life whom I have wanted to kill, mostly because they did not agree with the way I was thinking at the time.

Prayer

Dear God, when do we learn that life is precious? When do we learn that life is a gift from you? Why do I harbor ill will in my heart for other people? Please help me to…

My Thoughts: AR

While walking back from class, I was approached by two women who were trying to convert me to their religion. All I could think of was how I wish I'd never run into them. I couldn't even focus on what they were saying because all I was thinking was—how am I going to get away from this! Here they are pouring out their hearts to me and I couldn't reply to them or describe how my religion has helped my life. It in fact gives me life. I think I need to do more soul searching to be prepared to stand up for what I believe in. I also need to realize that they are people and I'm called to show love to them no matter who they are and to not give them the cold shoulder. I sure was giving them a bad message.

❧❧•❧❧

Thursday, Fifth Week of Lent

Genesis 17:3–9

God said to Abram, "You are to become the founder of a nation. From now on I will call you Abraham. I will be the only God you and your people will worship. I will give you all the land that you can see. For your part, you must follow my ways."

Psalm 105:4–9 *Follow God's way always*

Look to God for your strength. Serve God alone. Remember all the wonderful things God has done for us. God keeps the covenant.

John 8:51–59

Jesus said, "If you stay true to my words, you will never die." "Now we know he is crazy," the people listening said. "Everyone dies sometime, even our holy founder Abraham." Jesus responded, "I don't make these statements on my own. I get them from the very God you worship. In fact, *I* was, long before your founder existed." They couldn't believe what he was saying. They were so outraged they picked up stones to throw at him, but he got away first.

Further Reflection

It's funny how quickly people dismiss others because they don't agree with what that person has to say. The people in today's gospel story actually wanted to kill Jesus for what he said. There are some people in my life whom I don't want to associate with. Sometimes it's for a very good reason. Sometimes it's just because they don't agree with my way of thinking.

Prayer

Dear God, I need to be more accepting and tolerant of people who have different views than I do on life. I need to be more like your Son in the way he treated people. Please help me to...

My Thoughts: Tom Klein

Following God's way is not always easy. There are many temptations to stray from God's way of life, and it may often seem that we are forced to buck society in order to stay on his path. While we may temporarily become separated from the pathway of God, he is always there waiting for us and helping us to return to him.

❧❧●❧❧

Friday, Fifth Week of Lent

Jeremiah 20:10–13

Jeremiah couldn't believe it. Even his friends wanted him to fail. He felt God's presence in his life though. He handed his life over to God. Praise God. Praise God in song.

Psalm 18:2–7 *God hears my voice and answers me*

God, I love you with all my strength. You are my rock, my deliverer. Praise be to God in all things. Even when I'm in big trouble God is near to me. In my darkest moments I called on God and was heard.

John 10:31–42

"Why are you trying to stone me to death?" Jesus asked the people who were angry. "Is it something I did?" "It's not what you did, but what you said," they shouted back. "You think you're God, and we won't tolerate that kind of talk." Jesus replied, "I have said I am God's Son because I do God's bidding. I am in God and God is in me." They didn't appreciate his attempted explanation so they tried to have him arrested. He slipped out of their reach though.

Further Reflection

There are some people, no matter what they do or say, who don't seem to be able to please me. I can harbor some ugly thoughts about them. It probably reflects more on my attitude toward life than on the way these people are living theirs.

Prayer

Dear God, I can be so judgmental toward some people in my life. It's hard to even admit it, but I could use a change of attitude. Please help me to...

My Thoughts: David Klein

It is interesting that Jesus slipped out of the people's reach this time, but later he makes no attempt to save himself. I think this is significant because he knew what had to happen according to plan and this attempted arrest came too early. I don't think it is that bad to hold feelings against people who hurt you. Actually, it is bad, but very easy to do. If someone hurts you, it is easy to have hard feelings against him.

�֍•֍

Saturday, Fifth Week of Lent

Ezekiel 37:21–28

God said, "I will take Israel and make it a nation of my own. Never again shall it be divided. I will deliver them and cleanse them and make them my people. David shall be their shepherd and they will follow my ways. I will make with them a covenant of peace. I shall be with them forever.

(Psalm) Jeremiah 31:10–13 *God will shepherd us*

Listen to God's voice and follow it. God is our eternal shepherd. There will be plenty for everyone so rejoice now and always.

John 11:45–57

Many people believed in what Jesus had to say. Others thought he was a heretic who should be punished. Some people thought if he kept on, lots of others would follow him and then the Romans would come and destroy them all. They decided to figure out a way to kill Jesus so the Romans would not have a reason to put excess pressure on them all. They were sure they would get him soon, one way or the other.

Further Reflection

There is so much hate in the world. It's always been there. When will it stop? It will only stop when I am ready to rid my own heart of the hatred I have, which may be unspoken, but is still there.

Prayer

Dear God, I can harbor such ill feelings toward people for no good reason. Sometimes it's just bad chemistry. Whatever the excuse, it's not what you expect of me. Please help me to...

My Thoughts: Emily Miller

God tried to help get rid of the hate. There is too much in this world. We need to help get rid of that. I know that I will.

❧•❧

HOLY WEEK
Monday of Holy Week

Isaiah 42:1–7

God said, "This is one with whom I am really pleased. It is this person who will bring justice to the nations. This is my chosen one whom I have taken by the hand and formed and made a light to the nations and to those in need."

Psalm 27:1–3, 13–14 *God is my light and my salvation*

God is my refuge. There is nothing I need fear, even if there is trouble all around me, and people are out to get me. I believe I shall see the goodness of God, so I courageously wait for God.

John 12:1–11

Six days before the Passover, Jesus was having supper at this friend Lazarus's house. Mary came in the dining room and anointed the feet of Jesus with some expensive perfume. Judas was shocked. He thought the perfume should have been sold and the money used for the poor. (He really wanted the money for himself.) Jesus said, "Leave her alone. She's doing this in preparation for my burial. The poor will always be around. I won't be around much longer."

Further Reflection

Sometimes I think I'm a little like Judas. I say things to sound concerned, but deep down I have other motives that are not so altruistic. I need to mean what I say.

Prayer

Dear God, sometimes I can be such a phony. I say the right things but think and do the opposite. Help me not to be such a fraud. Please help me to…

My Thoughts: Jason Merkel

Think before I speak and may my words come from the heart. Amen.

Words are powerful. Often, I don't think people realize the power they are wielding when they speak, not only in what they choose to say, but even more so in what they choose not to. The difference between the two is a very fine line. Furthermore, discerning one side from the other is a task that is difficult for even the wisest of men, warranting even more caution for the rest of us trying to do it.

❧•❧

Tuesday of Holy Week

Isaiah 49:1–6

Isaiah said, "Listen to me. God called me from my beginning. Right from my mother's womb I was named. I was made God's servant here on earth. Even though it looks like I wasted my time, I really didn't, for I worked for God. My purpose was that I might draw you back to God's ways, that you might be a light to all the nations."

Psalm 71:1–6, 15, 17 *God, I will sing of your glory*

In you, God, I find my safety. Incline your ear to me. Help me. Be my surety, my stronghold in life. Save me from those who want to oppress me. You are my only hope. From my very beginning you are really the only one I trust. You're great, and I'll tell everyone I know how good you are.

John 13:21–23, 36–38

Jesus said to his friends, "One of you is going to betray me. I can feel it." His disciples were shocked. Peter asked, "Which one of us?" It was Judas Iscariot, but Jesus didn't say it openly to them all. To Judas he said, "Do what you're going to do quickly." Then Jesus said to his friends, "I'll be going back to God pretty soon. You'll look for me, but I won't be around. Right now you won't be able to follow me, but you will soon enough." Peter said, "I'd lay down my life for you." Jesus shook his head a little and said, "You'll deny me three times before that happens."

Further Reflection

If I were around, I would have never done what Peter did. I would have fought for Jesus to the end. But then I realize that even now I back off from doing the right thing all the time. I probably would have been in the same boat with Peter.

Prayer

Dear God, I need help in saying what I mean and meaning what I say. Sometimes I think and say all the right things, but then don't follow through on them. In some ways I'm a lot like Peter. Please help me to…

My Thoughts: David Klein

It's tough to stand up for what you believe in when your life is on the line, as Peter discovered. Yet, at the same time, if I was Peter, and Jesus said I would betray him, I would make a conscious effort not to.

❧❧●❧❧

Wednesday of Holy Week

Isaiah 50:4–9

Isaiah said, "God has given me the ability to speak clearly. I'm a good listener, too. I've been faithful to the one God I serve. I don't fight when people take advantage of me. I know God is a real help. I've really got nothing to worry about."

Psalm 69:8–10, 21–22, 31, 33–34 *God, answer me when I call out*

People shun me because I serve the one God. They laugh at me and make fun of me, but I don't care. I tell all of God's goodness and kindness.

Matthew 26:14–25

Judas went straight to the officials to inquire how much they would give him if he gave them the information they needed to arrest Jesus. When it got close to the celebration day of the Passover, Jesus had his friends go and get a room ready for them so they could eat together. During the meal Jesus said to them, "One of you is going to betray me, I know it." They all said, "Not me. I'd never do that." Even Judas protested, but they both knew what he intended to do.

Further Reflection

Sometimes I can say one thing and even make a big deal out of doing the right thing, yet know deep in my heart that as soon as I can, I'm going to do the very thing I said out loud I wouldn't. I may not be the cause of someone's death as Judas was, but I can kill people's reputations by the things I shouldn't have said in the first place (and said I wouldn't).

Prayer

Dear God, what we say and what we do have a real and sometimes hurtful impact on the people around us. I don't like deceit in other people. I hope I don't have any in my own life. Please help me to…

My Thoughts: Elizabeth R. Berning

It is so easy to say things we shouldn't say. At work I find myself talking about my coworkers in an unkind manner. I should try to be more patient and understanding of them. I should try to keep my thoughts to myself and say only good things.

SIX
WEEKDAYS OF THE EASTER SEASON

FIRST WEEK OF EASTER
Monday, First Week of Easter

Acts 2:14, 22–32

Peter stood up and talked to the people, "Listen to me. Jesus was raised from the dead. We can attest to the fact. We have witnesses who have talked with him."

Psalm 16:1–2, 5, 7–11 *God, I put all my trust in you*

God, you are my God. You mean everything to me. You are always in my thoughts. I feel good just knowing that you are there. Show me the right way to live.

Matthew 23:3–15

The women were on their way to tell the disciples everything they had seen, when from out of the blue Jesus appeared before them. "Peace," he said to them, "don't be afraid. Go and tell the others that I will see them in Galilee shortly." Meanwhile, back in the city, the guards who had been at the tomb were getting instructions from their superiors on how to lie when they were asked by anyone what had happened out at the tomb. They were paid off handsomely for the lies they would tell.

Further Reflection

They say everyone has their price. I can't imagine any amount being enough to deny that Jesus is Lord and Savior.

Prayer

Dear God, what a great gift I have in my faith. The apostles were so excited about it they told everyone they met how their faith in Jesus had changed their lives. My faith means a lot to me. Help me to…

My Thoughts: Brian Melody

Jesus asks us to believe in him and to show it by living his life. I can't imagine my best friends denying that they know me or denying their belief in me. I always try to put myself in Jesus' shoes.

Tuesday, First Week of Easter

Acts 2:36–41

Peter said to the people, "You must change your lives and be baptized in the name of Jesus, the risen Lord. Your sins will be forgiven and you will receive the gift of the Holy Spirit in your lives. This is an awful time and we need all the help from God we can get." That day over three thousand people were baptized.

Psalm 33:4–5, 18–20, 22 *God's goodness is all around us*

Hope and trust in God. God is just and right. God is our help and our protector. God will bless all who have hope.

John 20:11–18

As she was walking up to the tomb, Mary was in tears. She bent over and looked inside the place where Jesus had been buried. Two angels were inside. "Don't cry," one of them said. "I'm sad because I don't know where they took Jesus' body," she answered. Then she turned around and Jesus was standing by her. She didn't recognize him so she said. "If you're the one who took his body, tell me where it is so I can take proper care of it." Jesus answered, "Mary." At that instant she knew it was Jesus. She grabbed hold of him lovingly. "Go and tell the others that you've seen me," he said.

Further Reflection

Sadness turned to joy. Mary must have almost jumped out of her skin with excitement when she discovered that Jesus was alive. My faith should have the same effect on my life. I should be filled with joy that God has loved me so much.

Prayer

Dear God, what a gift I have in Jesus, your Son. It helps make sense out of what is sometimes a senseless world. Help me to…

My Thoughts: Annette Johnson

Help me to have the faith of Mary. Her eyes didn't see Jesus but that didn't stop her from believing that he was her son as well as the Son of God. Help me to believe in these people so completely that they never leave my mind. I do not understand this time. Help me not to need to. My mind cannot comprehend the things you have for me.

❧❧●❧❧

Wednesday, First Week of Easter

Acts 3:1–10

When Peter and John went up to the Temple to pray, they saw a crippled person being brought in at the same time. The crippled person asked Peter for some change. Peter said, "I don't have any money but what I do have I give to you. I command you in the name of Jesus to get up and walk." He got up immediately and everybody who was there was speechless at what they had just witnessed.

Psalm 105:1–4, 6–9 *God's goodness is all around us*

Let us give thanks to God. Let's tell everyone how good God is. Holy is God's name. God has chosen us and blessed us. God remembers the covenant forever.

Luke 24:13–35

Two people who knew Jesus were on their way to a town called Emmaus. They were talking about everything that had been happening when Jesus appeared on the road and started to walk with them. They didn't recognize him. He asked them what they were talking about. They figured he must be the only one for miles who had not heard about Jesus dying and rising from the dead. So they told him everything they had heard. When they finished, Jesus started to explain everything that had ever been prophesied about the Messiah. When they got to the village, Jesus acted like he was going on farther, but they insisted that he come in and have dinner with them.

When they sat down for supper Jesus took some bread and blessed it and gave it to them. It was then that they realized that they had been talking to Jesus. But then he vanished from their sight. They were so excited they didn't finish their meal but ran to tell the others whom they had seen and talked with.

Further Reflection

The disciples were beside themselves and had to go and tell others what they had experienced. I know that feeling. I've had joyful news that I just couldn't keep to myself. When I think of it, my faith is supposed to be that kind of joyful news.

Prayer

Dear God, what a gift you have given me in Jesus, our risen Lord. Give me the grace and the desire to share that good news with others. Please help me to…

My Thoughts: Elizabeth R. Berning

It seems as though sharing the good news is a good way to be ridiculed. The good news is good, though, and it should be shared, regardless of the outcome. Help me, Lord, to share your words and my faith with others.

❧❧•❧❧

Thursday, First Week of Easter

Acts 3:11–26

When a crowd formed around them to see the person who was cured, Peter asked, "What are you all looking at? The God of our ancestors who raised Jesus from the dead did this. It wasn't of our own doing. This is just a sign from God for you to reform your lives and turn back to God's ways. Believe in the power of Jesus the Lord."

Psalm 3:2, 5, 6–9 *God, how wonderful you are*

God, you are so good to us. We don't deserve your kindness. You have given our Savior dominion over everything that is.

Luke 24:35–43

Jesus came and stood in their midst and said, "Peace be with you." They were sure they were looking at a ghost but he let them touch his body to convince them he really was alive. He asked, "What do you have to eat? I'm hungry." Then he started to explain to them everything that was written about him in Scripture. He told them to go and preach to all about the forgiveness of sins.

Further Reflection

God truly has been good. I need to recognize the many gifts I have received from this all-loving God.

Prayer

Dear God, I have received so many blessings in my life. You have been so good and kind to me. Let me never forget. Please help me to…

My Thoughts: Kristin Nelson

Our God is truly a God of miracles. Curing the sick and raising Jesus from the dead are only two of the countless miracles our God has performed. Every day we are surrounded by them yet rarely take the time to notice them. What a wonderful world it would be if everyone was thankful to God for all the miracles surrounding them.

🌿•🌿

Friday, First Week of Easter

Acts 4:1–12

The officials were very angry at Peter and John for telling the people to believe in Jesus, so they had them arrested and thrown into jail. Even so, about 5,000 people were converted that day. The next day when Peter and John were brought before the court, Peter said, "I cured a sick person yesterday and I did it in the name of the risen Jesus. You can't change the facts. I suggest you believe in him too."

Psalm 118:1–2, 4, 22–27 *Christ is our foundation*

Let us give thanks to God. God is merciful and just. God takes that which is rejected and uses it as the cornerstone. Truly, this is the day God has blessed. God has shown us the way.

John 21:1–14

Peter and his friends were fishing all night long and caught nothing. Jesus was on shore and shouted to them, "Throw your nets off the other side of the boat and you'll catch something." They did and there were so many fish in their nets that they couldn't pull them back into the boat. "It's Jesus," John said to Peter. Peter was so excited to see Jesus he jumped into the water and swam to shore. The others brought the boat in as soon as they could. They caught over 150 fish. This was the third time Jesus appeared to his disciples after he was raised from the dead.

Further Reflection

Excitement, joy, peace, and love seem to be the feelings the disciples had whenever they talked about or experienced Jesus in their life.

Prayer

Dear God, you've been so good and kind to me. Sometimes I don't show my gratitude. Please help me to…

My Thoughts: Angela Becker

Realize that I must trust in you. It is sometimes hard to believe and put faith in your word when we cannot see or hear you. Give us the blind faith we need to live as you would. Although we cannot be perfect, help us to try each day. Help us to do your work in the face of adversity and objection.

❧❧•❧❧

Saturday, First Week of Easter

Acts 4:13–21

The officials were surprised at how at ease Peter and John were as they talked about Jesus in front of them. They told Peter that as part of their release, they were never to talk about Jesus again in public. But of course, that didn't stop them from proclaiming Jesus as Lord to all they saw and talked to.

Psalm 118:1, 14–21 *God always listens to our prayers*

Let's give thanks to God. God is our savior. God has been so good to us.

Mark 16:9–15

Jesus appeared to a lot of different people after he rose from the dead. He talked to Mary Magdalene and to the two on the road to Emmaus and to the eleven. He told them to go out and proclaim the good news of salvation to all they met.

Further Reflection

I've been given this good news, too. I have to do more with it than just cherish it in my heart. I, too, have to proclaim it to those I meet.

Prayer

Dear God, you have been so good and kind to me. Give me the courage and the strength to willingly proclaim the good news to people who come into my life. Please help me to...

My Thoughts: Chris Keyser

Sometimes, when we have a long-term goal, we lose sight of our objective. The reward for proclaiming God's word is a place in his kingdom. Sometimes we forget that God won't reward us until the end, and we neglect our duties.

❧❧•❧❧

SECOND WEEK OF EASTER
Monday, Second Week of Easter

Acts 4:23–31

After they were released from jail, Peter and John went back to the other disciples. They prayed for strength and were filled with the Holy Spirit. It gave them the courage to continue to preach about Jesus to anyone they met.

Psalm 2:1–9 *We trust in God*

Why do people refuse to follow God's ways? God will send one who will be able to rule the people. They will see the light and do what is right.

John 3:1–8

Nicodemus came to Jesus and said, "We really know that you are from God. We see all the wonderful things you are doing for people." Jesus responded, "You can enter God's reign only if you are born again of water and the Spirit."

Further Reflection

Both Jesus and the apostles talked about having God's Spirit in their lives. I guess if you're not doing good stuff, then you probably don't have God in your life.

Prayer

Dear God, I want to feel your presence in my life. I want your Spirit abiding in my life. I want to be helped to do what is right. I know I can't do it on my own. Please help me to…

My Thoughts: Amy Rybarczyk

Sometimes I think I can change people to include God more in their lives. I think if I set a good example or tell all the wonderful things the Lord has done for me, maybe they'll consider devoting more time to him. However, I've learned that one of the best things to do is to pray for people. I pray that the Holy Spirit will do the changing. He's obviously better at it than I'll ever be. Pray, hope and keep trying…that's the best I can do.

❧❀❧

Tuesday, Second Week of Easter

Acts 4:32–37

In the early Church, the community thought and acted as one. They threw everything they had into a common pot. People had their needs provided for. One person sold his whole farm and handed in all the proceeds from the sale.

Psalm 93:1–2, 5 *God is our ruler*

God is our ruler. It is God who created the world and all that is in it. God's reign is from the beginning of time. God's reign will last past the end of time. God's ways are trustworthy and true.

John 3:7–15

Jesus said to Nicodemus, "You have to be born of God's ways. You must believe in the one whom God has sent so that you can have eternal life."

Further Reflection

A lot of what Jesus says to Nicodemus is somewhat confusing. But I do know that I have to have God in my life if I am to have happiness in the life to come.

Prayer

Dear God, I want to please you in all things. I want to be with you for all eternity. Send me the help I need because I can't do it on my own. Please help me to…

My Thoughts: Elizabeth R. Berning

All we really have is God. God gives us what we need and through prayer he helps us with our day-to-day conflicts. Only God can save us.

❧❧•❧❧

Wednesday, Second Week of Easter

Acts 5:17–26

The Apostles were arrested and thrown into jail. During the night an angel from God came and let them out of jail. The next day they went right back to preaching about Jesus. When it was time for their appearance before the court, they were nowhere to be found, even though the jail locks were still in place. When the guards found them out preaching, they re-arrested them and brought them back without a fight.

Psalm 34:2–9 *God hears our prayers*

I always have a prayer on my lips. I always praise God for the goodness in my life. God always answers my prayers. Turn to God always. God hears us when we pray. Happy are those who trust in God's ways.

John 3:16–21

Jesus said to Nicodemus, "God so loved the world that the only Son was sent so that all who believe might have life forever. So follow God's ways and you will always live in the truth."

Further Reflection

It always amazes me that even though the apostles were thrown into jail for preaching about Jesus, as soon as they got out they went right back to preaching again. They truly had faith and believed that what Jesus promised them would come true if they were faithful.

Prayer

Dear God, give me the faith the apostles had. I want to always follow your ways. Please help me to…

My Thoughts: Joe Curry

Stay on the road of my faith journey. Through my words and actions in my daily life, help me live by the values of a true Christian.

Thursday, Second Week of Easter

Acts 5:27–33

When the apostles were in court, the judge said, "I told you not to be preaching about Jesus and you've disobeyed me." Peter answered, "We feel it's better to do what God wants us to do, rather than listen to what you tell us to do." The judge was not pleased with the way Peter talked to him.

Psalm 34:2, 9, 17–20 *God hears our prayers*

I always have a prayer on my lips. I always praise God for the goodness in my life. God always answers my prayers. Turn to God always. God hears us when we pray. Happy are those who trust in God's ways. God always helps us when we pray.

John 3:31–36

Jesus said to Nicodemus, "Whoever believes in the one whom God sent will have eternal life."

Further Reflection

To me, it took a lot of courage for the apostles to keep preaching about Jesus after they had been warned and even thrown into jail. I'd like to think I would do the same, but I sure wouldn't want to have to spend time in any jail.

Prayer

Dear God, I want to do your will. Help me to have the courage and strength that the apostles had. Please help me to…

My Thoughts: Nicole Borchardt

Lord, speak when you want me to speak, be silent when you want to be silent. Help me to know where to put my energy, what to change, and what to fight for. So often it happens, Lord, that you will bring difficulties into my life, and I want to run. Run away from this person, hide from that situation. God, help me to surrender myself completely to your will, help me to find you in everything (especially the trials!), and give me whatever it is I need to carry out your will.

❧❧●❧❧

Friday, Second Week of Easter

Acts 5:34–42

One of the judges said to the others, "I think we ought to downplay this whole Jesus stuff. If it is truly from God there is nothing we can do to stop it. If it's not from God, it'll dry up and blow away if we don't put too much emphasis on it." So they just whipped the apostles and let them go. But they didn't stop preaching about Jesus.

Psalm 27:1, 4, 13–14 *All my trust is in God*

God, you are everything to me. You give me courage and hope. All I want to do is please you. I want to be with you forever.

John 6:1–15

One day Jesus went up on the side of a hill and started to teach the people who had followed him there. After a while he felt sorry for them because they were a long way from town and they were getting hungry. Jesus asked Philip, "Where can we get some food to feed these people?" Philip laughed and said, "We couldn't feed all these people if we had two days wages among us."

One of the other followers said, "There's someone here who has five fish and two loaves of bread. But that's a drop in the bucket compared to what we'd need to feed all these people." "Get the people to sit down on the grass," Jesus said. Then he took the fish and bread, gave thanks to God, broke them into pieces, and passed them out to the people to eat. Everyone ate until they were full. When they were all done, there were at least twelve baskets of food left over. There were over five thousand people who were fed.

Further Reflection

Jesus helped the whole person. He didn't just give people nice words to live by. He helped them in all of their needs, whether it was hunger, or sickness, or even bringing people back from the dead. I like to think I reach out to people whatever their need may be.

Prayer

Dear God, sometimes I just want to be left alone so I can spend all my time praying to you. That's not what your Son Jesus did. Please help me to…

My Thoughts: Annette Johnson

Help me to realize my own potential! I always thought that a life of constant prayer was what God wanted. I actually get to do stuff!!!!

❧❧•❧❧

Saturday, Second Week of Easter

Acts 14:22–33

Lots of people became Christians but with so many people to instruct, some of the widows got overlooked and weren't getting their share of the food. So they selected twelve people to be deacons who took over the task of overseeing the welfare of the communities while the apostles took care of the spiritual matters.

Psalm 33:1–2, 4–5, 18–19 *God, we really trust in you*

Let's give thanks to God with all our hearts. God is trustworthy and full of kindness. God will protect us.

John 6:16–21

One night while the apostles were crossing the lake in their boat, a sudden storm came up and they were scared for their lives. Just as they were about to give up all hope, they saw Jesus coming toward them. He said, "Don't be afraid." Then all of a sudden they made it to shore safely.

Further Reflection

It's kind of interesting. When I place my trust and hope in God, things in my life don't seem so unmanageable.

Prayer

Dear God, there have been many storms in my life. They've been quelled when I hand it all over to you. Please help me to…

My Thoughts: Kortney Jendro

There are so many things to do, and our world is becoming more complicated every day. Sometimes it can seem too much. Sometimes we no longer can manage on our own. The weight of living becomes unbearable. That is what you place in his hands: all those trivialities that add up. Just offer it all up to Him.

THIRD WEEK OF EASTER
Monday, Third Week of Easter

Acts 6:8–15

Stephen was a good believer in Jesus. He went around helping lots of people. Lots of people were jealous of all the good he was doing. They came up with some trumped-up charges and had him taken to court. Whatever they said about him in court didn't seem to have an effect on him. None of it bothered him because he believed.

Psalm 119:23–27, 29–30 *Blest are those who try to lead a life full of goodness*

God, help me to know and follow your ways. I don't care what other people think or say. I want to follow your true ways.

John 6:22–29

One night the disciples of Jesus sailed across the lake to the other side. While they were in the middle of the lake, a huge and violent storm came up and they were caught in it. Out of nowhere Jesus came near the boat and said, "Don't be afraid." Then before they knew it, their boat was safe on the other side of the lake. No one was harmed.

Further Reflection

I've been in some tough spots like the disciples and Stephen were in. And like them it was only by the grace of God that I came through unscathed.

Prayer

Dear God, don't ever be far from me. You are the very strength that keeps me going. Please help me to…

My Thoughts: Amy Rybarczyk

It's definitely a daunting task to live out the truth in today's society. It seems at times everything and everyone tries to pull me in directions that take me away from the truth. It's like most people want me to be everything opposite of what the Lord asks. I often get involved with the "wrong crowd," which leads me to do things that offend the Lord. The devil is very good at tempting me and making evil things or situations look appealing. Doing good acts seem to cause so much humiliation—what God calls us to do, but what the "wrong crowd" discourages. It seems that selfish, prideful acts are praised in the majority of society. It's a great blessing when I find people who have a positive effect on my life and lead me to the truth!

❧❧•❧❧

Tuesday, Third Week of Easter

Acts 7:51—8:1

Stephen stood up in court to defend himself. He said, "You are all pretty cold-hearted people. Even some of your ancestors didn't listen to the prophets when they spoke. You have a long history of being close-minded." The court officials didn't like what Stephen was saying. They were so mad they took him out of the city and stoned him. Just before he died he prayed, "God, take me to yourself and don't hold this against them."

Psalm 31:3–4, 6–8, 17, 21 *God, all my hope is in you*

God, you are everything to me. Help me and show me the way. I trust you.

John 6:30–35

The people wanted Jesus to perform a miracle for them. They said, "Give us some food to eat like Moses did for the people a long time ago." "You're a hard bunch to please. I don't do those things on my own. Moses didn't perform those miracles. It was God who sent the food down from heaven." "Well, give us that food then." Jesus said, "To be honest with you, I am the food. I am the bread of life. Anyone who believes in me will never go hungry again."

Further Reflection

These two stories make me appreciate all the more the real blessing I have that I can receive Jesus' help and himself in the Eucharist. Stephen gave up his life believing in Jesus. Jesus offers us life everlasting if we just believe.

Prayer

Dear God, I believe in your Son. Give me the strength to live that belief every day of my life. Please help me to…

My Thoughts: Steve Jaeger

These passages demonstrate how many have difficulty believing without proof. It also shows how some refuse to believe even when there is proof of God through Jesus. As it was common then, it is likely just as common now. Although many don't believe, we should not give up strength in our belief.

❧❧•❧❧

Wednesday, Third Week of Easter

Acts 8:1–8

Even though people like Saul persecuted the apostles and disciples of Jesus, they kept on believing and acting in the name of Jesus.

Psalm 66:1–7 *Let the whole world shout to God with joy*

Praise God. Praise God's name. God is so good to us. God's goodness will never end.

John 6:35–40

Jesus said, "I am the bread of life. Anyone who believes in me shall never go hungry again. I am here because this is what God wants me to do. If you follow my way, you'll have eternal life."

Further Reflection

The apostles believed Jesus was the way to eternal life. They gave up their lives rather than stop believing in Jesus. I want what they have.

Prayer

Dear God, I want to do what you want me to do. Jesus says it's doing it his way. Help me to do just that. Please help me to…

My Thoughts: Amy Rybarczyk

If God forgot about me for one minute…I'd cease to exist! God loves me and can't stop loving me. He's the only one who can love me with a perfect love. I need to keep reminding myself of these things I've been taught over the years, especially when I'm being persecuted or having any sort of trouble, downfall, or discouragement. My day seems to get less burdensome if I remember these things. Life is easier when I have someone to believe in—Jesus—and when I have something to look forward to—eternal life.

✿❦•❦✿

Thursday, Third Week of Easter

Acts 8:26–40

Philip met an important person from Ethiopia who was reading from the book of Isaiah. He didn't really understand what it was all about, so Philip gave him some instructions. He pointed out how many of the things that Isaiah prophesied about were fulfilled in the person of Jesus. The Ethiopian was so moved that Philip baptized him right then and there.

Psalm 66:8–9, 16–17, 20 *Let the whole world shout to God with joy*

Praise God. Praise God's name. God is so good to us. God gave us our very lives. God's goodness will never end.

John 6:44–51

Jesus said, "If you believe in me, you will have eternal life. I am the bread of life come down from heaven."

Further Reflection

What a blessed life I have. Not only has God given me the very breath I breathe, everything I have comes from God. What a blessing I have in the Eucharist. Jesus really is the bread of life.

Prayer

Dear God, you have been so good to me. Please help me to...

My Thoughts: Elizabeth R. Berning

Christ's love is so amazing. Help me to try to be more appreciative and awestruck by it.

❧•❧

Friday, Third Week of Easter

Acts 9:1–20

Saul was passionate about persecuting Christians. Then one day he was knocked to the ground by a lightening blast from the sky. While he was on the ground he heard a voice say, "Why are you persecuting me?" Saul asked who the voice was. The response was, "It is I, Jesus. Go into the city and I'll tell you what to do then." Saul did as he was instructed, even though he was blinded by the event. He went to a holy man named Ananias who reluctantly gave him his eyesight back because he was instructed to do so in a vision. Saul was baptized and then began preaching the good news in the synagogues.

Psalm 117:1–2 *Proclaim the good news*

Everyone praise God. Give glory to God with all you have. Spread the good news.

John 6:52–59

The people didn't understand what Jesus was talking about. They wondered what he meant about eating his flesh. Jesus said, "If you eat my flesh and drink my blood, you will have life eternal. Just as God has given me life, so I will give you life."

Further Reflection

Jesus is the answer. It seems so natural to believe in him. And yet like Saul, sometimes we need a stiff jolt to help that reality sink in.

Prayer

Dear God, I don't like pain. Please make it easier to continue to believe in your Son without getting struck down like Saul did. Please help me to...

My Thoughts: Annette Johnson

Help me break down any walls that keep out love before the walls lock me inside. Protect me as I find a job. Help me to be worthy of doing something for your good. Keep me from chasing large amounts of money. Continually remind me that my riches are in heaven. Help me to stay committed to spreading the confidence of your peace rather than the darkness of doubt. Help me to surround myself with people who will reinforce my faith and challenge me to follow my beliefs with my behavior. Help us to help each other.

❦●❦

Saturday, Third Week of Easter

Acts 9:31–42

One day while Peter was traveling around, he came across a person who was crippled and had been bedridden for eight years. In the name of Jesus, Peter cured him. The man became a faithful follower. In another town about the same time, there was a lady who was a faithful, practicing Christian. She was always helping others. She died suddenly. While they were preparing her body to be buried, Peter came to pay his respects. He was so moved by the stories he heard of her good life that he said to her, "Stand up." It was a miracle they talked about for years. She spent the rest of her life helping others.

Psalm 116:12–17 *God has been so good to me*

How can I ever repay God for all the good I've received? Praised be God's name. God, I have come to do your will. I thank you for your goodness and praise you every day.

John 6:60–69

Some of the disciples were finding the things Jesus was saying not easy to accept. He said to them, "My words are spirit and life. Yet I know that's hard for some of you to believe. Belief in me is really a gift from God." Some of them drifted away, never to return. But the twelve stuck with him. Peter, in a way only he could say, said, "Jesus, where would we go if we left you?"

Further Reflection

Sometimes I wish I could see some of those miracles that Peter performed for people. It would be so much easier to believe if I saw something unexpected happen, something miraculous, happen. Then I realize there are all sorts of miraculous things happening in my very life right now for which I am very thankful. Besides, where else would I go?

Prayer

Dear God, your Son has the words of life. Help me to live those words every waking moment of my day. Please help me to...

My Thoughts: Jenny Tomes

Seeing is believing. Blind faith. There have been so many times in my life when I've requested for a lightning bolt to strike down, reassuring me of God's presence. But as I've grown, I've discovered God's presence in more appropriate bolts: family, friends, strangers, mature music, and knowledge. If I were to combine all God's miracles that I've experienced, I'd have one mammoth bolt. God gives me only what I can handle—and plenty of opportunities to be restruck by His wonder.

❧ • ❧

FOURTH WEEK OF EASTER
Monday, Fourth Week of Easter

Acts 11:1–18

After the Gentiles started to be accepted as followers of Christ, some of the people started to grumble about letting them in. Peter went to see if there was anything he could do about the situation. "I had a vision one night," Peter said. "I saw a blanket come down out of the sky. It had all kinds of animals on it, even pigs. God said, 'Kill the animals and eat them for food. Nothing I have created is bad. It's all good.' This dream happened three times in a row. The next day," Peter continued, "some people took me to a home of a Gentile who told me he, too, had a dream and was instructed to talk to me and learn how to be saved. As I was talking to them, the Spirit of God descended upon us right then and there. Then I remembered Jesus telling us to baptize with the Holy Spirit." The grumblers knew this truly was a sign from God so they stopped their bickering.

Psalm 42:2–3; 43:3–4 *I long to be with God*

God, I need you in my life. God, I want you in my life. Show me the way. I want to spend my whole life worshiping you and doing your will.

John 10:1–10

Jesus said, "I am the way. If you follow me, you'll have true life abundantly."

Further Reflection

I grumble a lot when things don't go my way. Sometimes I feel I know all the answers and everybody should do it "my way." Peter pointed out to the grumblers of his time that there is a "way" and it's really God's way.

Prayer

Dear God, so often I want to do things my way, and I forget about the feelings and the dignity and worth of the people around me. Give me the strength to see things your way. Please help me to...

My Thoughts: Zach Czaia

In my life, I must be ready to respond to the voice of the Good Shepherd. If I am a sheep, I must be a good sheep. A good sheep recognizes instantly the call of his master, as Peter recognized instantly the Holy Spirit behind the "blanket in the sky" vision. If I want to have that instant response, that quickening to the word of God, I must remove these obstacles, which get in the way of God's message. I must clean the wax from my sheep's ears, so when he calls, I will respond. What is the wax? The wax is attachment to things of this world: attachment to the body, to pleasures, to the worries of the world, and to my daily life. But I must remember that these things are not wax in themselves. The body and its pleasures, the mind and its faculties are gifts from God. I must have them (as David says in the psalms) to praise him. If we are finding ways to use our gifts for others and for God, then our heart and ears will be supple listening to the word of God. I pray for the wisdom to use my gifts in a way that pleases God and for the courage to detach from the things of this world, which get in the way of my relationship with Him.

❧❧●❧❧

Tuesday, Fourth Week of Easter

Acts 11:19–26

A large number of Greeks were converted into believing in Jesus and his way of life. So Barnabas went to Antioch and spent a year instructing them and encouraging them to remain faithful to Jesus. It was here that the term *Christian* was first used to describe followers of Jesus.

Psalm 87:1–7 *Everyone, praise God*

God, you are truly great. Everyone should know that you are the one who created everything that is or will be. Everyone should sing your praises, for you are wonderful.

John 10:22–30

Some people came up to Jesus and asked, "Are you the Messiah or what?" Jesus said, "I've already told you but you won't even believe after everything you've seen me do in God's name. People who really know me believe in me. I give them eternal life because God and I are one."

Further Reflection

Sometimes I take my faith in Jesus for granted. It meant a lot to the converts in the early days of Christianity. I should be more aware of what a great and precious gift it is.

Prayer

Dear God, belief in your Son means eternal life. It seems so far away that it loses its importance in my life. Help me to be aware that eternity with you is only one breath away. Please help me to...

My Thoughts: Tom Klein

It is amazing to think that the entire religion we believe in—even its name—was started by one man who lived so long ago. Even when the term *Christian* came about, it was Barnabas who said the term to a select group of people, but now it is one of the predominant religions in the world.

❧❀❧

Wednesday, Fourth Week of Easter

Acts 12:24—13:5

One day during prayer, the Holy Spirit spoke to those present in the room, saying, "I need Barnabas and Paul to do some special work for me." So they prayed for them and designated them special by putting their hands on them, and then sent them off as the Spirit instructed. Through their preaching, the word of God really spread far and wide.

Psalm 67:2–3, 5–6, 8 *Everyone, praise God*

God, help us and save us. Let your kindness smile upon us. You are a wonderful God who rules fairly.

John 12:44–50

Jesus said, "Whoever believes in me believes also in God who sent me here. God has instructed me to say what I say. I offer you eternal life if you believe in me."

Further Reflection

I believe, but sometimes I don't feel it has much of an impact on my daily life. I often feel I should be doing more. Using my faith doesn't mean I have to go around the world preaching like Paul and Barnabas did. Using my faith can simply mean having a better attitude toward the things and people placed in my everyday life.

Prayer

Dear God, sometimes I think you want so much from me that I get weighted down just thinking about all the things I should be doing. Help me to take life one day at a time and to do the best with what I'm given each moment. Please help me to...

My Thoughts: Will French

These readings are all about faith and believing in God. Faith comes in many different forms. One can use our faith in many different ways, from going out and spreading the word of God to letting it govern the way we perceive and act toward the people and events we encounter every day.

❧●❧

Thursday, Fourth Week of Easter

Acts 13:13–25

One day while Paul was in the synagogue, the people asked him to speak to them. Paul said, "The God you worship has done great things for you. You were saved from slavery and led out to this land you live in. You've been given some good rules to help lead you in God's ways. David was one of the greatest of kings. I believe that Jesus, who comes from David's family, was sent to be our Messiah. John the Baptist, who was respected by a lot of people, even thought this was so. That's what he preached and even pointed out Jesus to people he was working with."

Psalm 89:2–3, 21–22, 25, 27 *God's goodness lasts forever*

I will spread the news of how good God has been to everyone who will listen. God has always loved us like family. God, you mean everything to us.

John 13:16–20

Jesus said, "You'll be blessed if you practice what I have taught you. You can believe me because I am the ONE whom God sent."

Further Reflection

What a blessing it is to have God in our lives. How often I get caught up in so many things and forget what a blessing I have.

Prayer

Dear God, thank you for being in my life. It makes all the difference. Please help me to...

My Thoughts: David Klein

Paul's lecture was simply a persuasive speech convincing the Jews that Jesus is the Messiah. Fortunately, we believe simply by faith without having to be persuaded to believe.

❧❧•❧❧

Friday, Fourth Week of Easter

Acts 13:26–33

Paul said to the people, "This was the message that God intended for all of us to hear but some refused to listen. In fact, there were some who were extremely jealous of all that Jesus did and said. Jesus was actually killed but he rose on the third day through the power of the most high God that we all worship. That's why I'm telling you about this good news."

Psalm 2:6–11 *You are a child of mine*

I tell you all, even rulers, heed what God tells us to do. Serve God with all you have. We owe everything to God's goodness.

John 14:1–6

Jesus said, "Don't worry. Believe in God and in me. I am going to prepare you a place. In God's house, there are many rooms. Then I'll come back and take you with me. Actually, you know the way." Thomas said, "Jesus, we don't know where you're going. How can we know the way?" Jesus replied, "I am the way."

Further Reflection

Sometimes we let life get so confusing. We make life more complicated than it really needs to be. Jesus is the way. And his way is pretty well spelled out. We're to love God and love those around us.

Prayer

Dear God, help me to do your will in all the things I do. Don't let me get sidetracked. Please help me to...

My Thoughts: Dave Klein

Jesus is merely trying to stress the trust in him that is necessary to be saved. By believing and living for God, we will be able to follow Jesus and he will take us to life everlasting.

❧❧•❧❧

Saturday, Fourth Week of Easter

Acts 13:44–52

One day a lot of people from town came to hear what Paul and Barnabas had to say. The other people got very jealous. They became verbally abusive. Paul said, "Look, it's no skin off my nose if you don't want to listen to what we have to say. There are a lot of people who really appreciate what we're offering." So before trouble broke out, Paul and Barnabas left town for another place where they knew the people would be more receptive.

Psalm 98:1–4 *Wherever one is, God's saving power is present*

Let's sing a song to God. God's goodness is all about us. No matter where one looks, God's love is present. Be happy and glad.

John 14:7–14

Jesus said, "To know me is to know who God is. I am in God and God is in me. If you believe in me you will be able to do great things. Just ask and it will be given to you."

Further Reflection

Sometimes I act like the people in the first reading. I choose not to follow what Jesus has laid out for me to do with my life. Sometimes I choose to go the other way. Sometimes I sin. I suspect if I really worked on knowing Jesus, I'd have less reason to stray.

Prayer

Dear God, I don't like it when I stray far from you and the way Jesus has pointed out for me. Give me the strength not only to know your will, but the grace to live it out in my life. Please help me to...

My Thoughts: Kristin Nelson

The reflection makes me realize what little time I spend trying to know Jesus. I am so easily distracted by other things, such as sleep, school, TV, and other stuff, none of which matters for my salvation. In order to fix this I should set aside time in my schedule specifically for God.

❧•❧

FIFTH WEEK OF EASTER
Monday, Fifth Week of Easter

Acts 14:5–18

Word got out that some people were going to try to kill Paul and Barnabas, so they hightailed it out of town and went to preach somewhere else. When they arrived at Lystra, Paul cured a man who was crippled. He simply told him to "get up," and he did. The people were so impressed that they started calling Paul and Barnabas gods. Paul and Barnabas pointed out that they were merely humans who were trying to do God's will in their lives. Many of the people still believed that Paul and Barnabas were gods though.

Psalm 115:1–4, 15–16 *God, to you we give all honor and glory*

Nothing really comes from us. It is all God's doing. God, you alone are great and wonderful.

John 14:21–26

Jesus said, "If you follow my commands, you will be loved by God. In fact, God and I will dwell in you. I'll send the Spirit to you soon so you will be able to understand everything I have told you."

Further Reflection

Sometimes I get pretty puffed up in the head and start to think I'm pretty important and cause all sorts of wonderful things to happen. When I get that way I need to be reminded to pray a little more and thank God for all the wonderful things that have happened in my life because of God's grace.

Prayer

Dear God, without you I can do nothing. Please let me give credit where credit is due. Please help me to…

My Thoughts: Tom Klein

This reminds me of the fact that God works through us to touch the world. All the good inside of us comes directly from God, who gives us the ability to do good deeds through the use of his gifts. As we do good deeds, it is equally important for us to thank God for the ability to have done so.

🙚•🙘

Tuesday, Fifth Week of Easter

Acts 14:19–28

Some of the people who were angry with Paul stoned him and left him for dead. His wounds looked worse than they were. The next day he and Barnabas left and went to another town called Derbe. They were a great success there and had many converts. They traveled all over, encouraging the newly formed communities to keep the faith.

Psalm 145:10–13, 21 *God, we all recognize how good you have been to us*

God, we bless you and your name. We talk about your goodness wherever we go. You've got all the deep answers for life's questions. I want to shout your praises out loud.

John 14:27–31

Jesus said, "I wish you peace. That's my gift to you. Don't worry. I'm going to a better place, but one day I'll come back for you."

Further Reflection

One of the things that impresses me about the early disciples is that no matter what happened in their lives, they kept doing what they were called to do. Paul was beaten up and left for dead. Yet, when he discovered his wounds weren't so bad, instead of leaving the ministry for a more sedate life, he went right back to preaching the good news, the very thing that got him into trouble in the first place.

Prayer

Dear God, give me the courage and the faith that people like Paul had. I could be a better witness to the love you have for the world and the people in it. Please help me to…

My Thoughts: David Klein

I wish I had the determination and inner drive that Paul had. When people put me down or I have failed at something, I always get back up as Paul did, but I find it hard to remain focused on my course and continue on as Paul did. It takes great devotion to do what he did.

❧❧•❧❧

Wednesday, Fifth Week of Easter

Acts 15:1–6

There was a big argument brewing among the different communities about whether men had to be circumcised or not. Paul and Barnabas went to Peter and the other apostles to discuss the problem.

Psalm 122:1–5 *It's always wonderful to feel God's closeness*

It's wonderful to go up to the holy city. That's where one of the most beautiful Temples to God is. It is an ancient and holy place.

John 15:1–8

Jesus said, "I am the trunk of the tree. God is the gardener. God prunes and hoes and tends to the tree so that it yields much fruit. Live on in me, for I will give you life and you will bear much fruit."

Further Reflection

When Paul came upon a problem, he sought advice from the apostles. Sometimes I think I can do it all by myself, though I've discovered when I get a consensus of opinion on some matter, the solution is easier to come by.

Prayer

Dear God, give me the wisdom to seek advice when I'm at a juncture in my life. Sometimes I think I can handle anything, but that's usually a big front. I need as much help as I can get. Give me the courage to ask. Please help me to…

My Thoughts: Emily Miller

Paul asked for help when there was a problem. All you have to do is ask God for help if you need it.

❧❧•❧❧

Thursday, Fifth Week of Easter

Acts 15:7–21

After a lengthy and heated discussion, Peter took the floor and said, "It seems to me that circumcision is a local custom and not a universal reality. People are becoming Christians because of faith in Jesus and his way. We shouldn't be burdening people with incidentals to that faith. They should assimilate our beliefs, not our local customs. They have their own."

Psalm 96:1–3, 10 *God has been wonderful to all of us*

Let's make up a new song to proclaim to all the people how wonderful God is. Let's announce it wide and far. Our God is a wonderful and great God.

John 15:9–11

Jesus said, "I love you as much as God loves me. The only thing I ask of you is that you keep my commandment of loving those around you. Then you will know true happiness."

Further Reflection

It's interesting that sometimes we put people through all kinds of hoops to make sure they are worthy. We do it in organizations. We do it in fraternities. The early Church came up with their own set of regulations. I think our faith actually teaches us to be more accepting and open.

Prayer

Dear God, let me treat others exactly the way I would like to be treated in return. Please help me to…

My Thoughts: Jason Merkel

God, help me see my own faults. I am not perfect—you know that more than anybody—and for me to expect or demand perfection from others is wrong. Everyone has his or her own beliefs and ideas. Help me to accept them with an open mind, and not to belittle anybody because they are different from me. Dear Lord, we are all your people. Help me accept others into my life as I am trying to accept you.

❧❧●❧❧

Friday, Fifth Week of Easter

Acts 15:22–31

The apostles decided to send reps with Paul and Barnabas to tell the people about their decision not to burden people with circumcision, if that wasn't part of their local customs. It was a relief to most of the men to hear that news.

Psalm 57:8–12 *God, I will praise you always and everywhere*

I will sing a song to praise my God. God, I give you thanks and praise every day. You are by far the greatest.

John 15:12–17

Jesus said to the disciples, "1 want you to love one another. There is no greater act than to give up one's life for another person. You will be my close friends if you willingly do what I ask of you. I guarantee you this, if you love one another, you will bear much fruit."

Further Reflection

Concern for others—that doesn't seem like much to ask from a God who has given everything to us already. I don't know why it's so hard to follow through on.

Prayer

Dear God, give me the strength and the desire and the will to live my life in accord with your wishes. Even if it takes a miracle, I want to love as you want me to. Please help me to…

My Thoughts: David Klein

What is the significance of circumcision? It's too bad Peter didn't lay his life down for Jesus because there would have been no greater act, especially because it was the Son of Man and not just an ordinary person.

Saturday, Fifth Week of Easter

Acts 16:1–10

Paul took Timothy with him on many trips to preach the good news. They went everywhere together.

Psalm 100:1–3, 5 *God is good to us*

Let us all sing songs of joy to God. God has done everything for us. God is so good to us.

John 15:18–21

Jesus said, "I have chosen you to be special. Don't worry if people don't understand you or like you."

Further Reflection

Paul had a good idea to take Timothy with him on the preaching trips he made. We all need help and a friend to share our lives with. Even Jesus gathered a few chosen friends around him in his ministry.

Prayer

Dear God, Jesus needed friends. Paul needed a friend. Help me never to think I can do it on my own. Please help me to…

My Thoughts: Anonymous

Sometimes I don't realize how wonderful my friends are. When they call me on things in order to help me to grow, I definitely need to be more open to them instead of getting offended. I'm glad my friends come back to me even after I push them away or do things that hurt them. Forgiveness is a wonderful gift. Sometimes I think I don't need friends—that all I need is God. However, I know he brings people in my life to help me get closer to him. Some friends seem to have a negative influence on me, but I suppose it's my role to help them find God and to be an example to them.

❧❧•❧❧

SIXTH WEEK OF EASTER
Monday, Sixth Week of Easter

Acts 16:11–15

On one of his trips, Paul met up with some people who gathered near a riverbank. One of the people in the crowd was a woman who sold costly purple cloth. She was really touched by what Paul had to say, so they baptized her along with all the people from her household. Afterward, she insisted that Paul and his friends stay at her house while they were in the area preaching.

Psalm 149:1–6, 9 *God really loves us*

Let's sing a song to God. God made us. We're so thankful. Let's never stop thanking God for being so good to us.

John 15:26—16:4

Jesus said, "When the Spirit of God comes upon you, more things will be revealed to you. Don't worry. Don't let your faith be shaken. People won't like you and will hurt you because of what you believe in, but in the long run they really can't hurt you."

Further Reflection

I want everyone to like me, but that's never really going to happen. Some people will actually walk across the street to avoid me when they know that I am a believer in Christ. It's real funny in a sense, because my faith is what sets me free. I hope I never lose that perspective on life.

Prayer

Dear God, how blessed I am to have been given the precious gift of faith in you. Strengthen that faith with the gifts of your Holy Spirit in my life. Please help me to…

My Thoughts: Brian Melody

I feel that the world would be a very scary place without God. When a nonbeliever dies does their life end that day? Believers in God live happily forever.

❧❧•❧❧

Tuesday, Sixth Week of Easter

Acts 16:22–34

Paul and Silas were thrown into jail. They spent their time preaching and encouraging the other prisoners. One night an earthquake shook the whole area. The jail was left wide open. The jailer was sure the prisoners had all escaped and was going to kill himself rather than have to face his superiors with the bad news. But Paul spoke up before he had a chance to kill himself. The jailer was so relieved he asked Paul what he must do to be saved. "Believe in Jesus," Paul responded. That day the jailer and his whole household were baptized.

Psalm 138:1–3, 7–8 *God, you have been so good to us*

God, we thank you for all you've done for us. Bless you forever and ever. You've always listened to me when I've called upon you for help. May your goodness and kindness last forever.

John 16:5–11

Jesus said, "I know you are sad that I'm going to leave you soon. But I need to so that I can send God's Spirit back to be with you."

Further Reflection

There are times when I wish Jesus was physically present to me to point the way. I realize, though, that God's Spirit is always present to me just like Jesus promised the apostles. I'm never alone, no matter what. God truly is good to us.

Prayer

Dear God, what a wonderful and kind God you are. Your Spirit is always in my life, giving me the strength and grace to do the things I need to do to please you. Please help me to…

My Thoughts: Elizabeth R. Berning

God is always with me no matter what happens. His Spirit surrounds me and I am blessed. There have been many times when I have faltered, but it is the Holy Spirit working in others and me that has helped me to continue on the right path.

❧❧●❧❧

Wednesday, Sixth Week of Easter

Acts 17:15, 22—18:1

Paul was in Athens preaching. He stood up in a place called the Areopagus and spoke to the people. He said, "I can see that you are very religious people. You have altars to all sorts of gods. You even have an altar to the Unknown God. I suggest to you that this Unknown God is really the God that I worship." Then he told them how God had created the world and peopled it, and how Jesus, the only Son, came to earth to redeem us from our sins. A few people were very impressed with what he said and were baptized. A lot weren't.

Psalm 148:1–2, 11–14 *God, the whole world is a sign of your goodness*

Praise God for all the goodness that has been showered upon us. Rulers, praise God. Important people, praise God. Ordinary people, praise God. Everyone, praise God. God has been so good to us.

John 16:12–15

Jesus said, "I've got a lot more to tell you, but the time is not right now. The Spirit that I send after I'm gone will tell you the rest. Everything you learn from the Spirit is right from the mouth of God, so believe everything you're told."

Further Reflection

For Jesus, God's Spirit seems to have been an important part of his life. I need to spend more time in prayer to this Spirit, asking for help in living my life. The Spirit is full of wisdom and power and strength and grace. I need all of these things in my life.

Prayer

Dear God, send me your Holy Spirit that I may see things more as you would have me see them. Please help me to…

My Thoughts: Annette Johnson

Please help me to recognize and acknowledge the Holy Spirit. Help me to be stripped of my own selfish inner voices.

❦❧•❦❧

Thursday, Sixth Week of Easter

Acts 18:1–8

Paul went to Corinth. He met Aquila and his wife Priscilla, who had recently been expelled from Rome. Paul moved in with them and they made tents together for a place to live. On the Sabbath Paul would lead discussions in the synagogue. Not everybody liked what he had to say. He finally got so upset with them that he decided to work only with Gentiles. Over time many from that town became Christians.

Psalm 98:1–4 *God's salvation is ours*

Let's sing songs to God for all the great things God has done for us. God is faithful and kind. How blessed we've been.

John 16:16–20

Jesus said, "Very soon you won't see me anymore. And then later you will." The disciples didn't really know what that meant. Jesus knew they were confused so he said, "Soon it will be time for mourning, but then that mourning will be turned to joy."

Further Reflection

Sometimes when I read stories from the Bible, I don't fully understand what they are saying. It's always handy to have a dictionary of the Bible and a simple concordance next to my Bible so I can look up some of those confusing passages and get a better understanding of their meaning.

Prayer

Dear God, thank you for the Bible scholars in this world who can help me understand your living word in the books they have written about different parts of the Bible. Please help me to…

My Thoughts: Kristin Nelson

Jesus spoke in parables for a reason. That way anyone who truly wanted to know the meaning in what he said had to pray for wisdom and seek him with their entire hearts. It is nice to have wise people to translate some confusing words of God, but at the same time we too should seek Jesus with our entire hearts and then we will be brought from darkness to light; from confusion to understanding.

My Thoughts: Annette Johnson

Help me to be less proud with my intelligence. Help me to have faith in other people's work. It is getting exhausting to doubt so much.

❧❧●❧❧

Friday, Sixth Week of Easter

Acts 18:9–18

One night Paul had a vision in his sleep. Jesus told him not to worry or be afraid because he would be accepted by the people while he preached in Corinth. He was brought to court once while he was there, but they quickly dropped the charges. After about a year of preaching there, he moved on to Syria. It was then that he shaved his head because of a vow he had made.

Psalm 47:2–7 *God is creator and ruler of all the earth*

Clap your hands and shout for joy because God has been so good to us. Sing and sing and sing it with all your heart and soul.

John 16:20–23

Jesus said, "For a while you'll be sad, but that will eventually turn to joy. I'm leaving soon, but I'll be back one day."

Further Reflection

It's sad when people I love move on. I think I know how the apostles must have felt when Jesus told them he was going away. I'm glad he promised and sent the Spirit to fill in for him.

Prayer

Dear God, never be far from me. Life is hard enough. I can't imagine what it would be like without your help. Please help me to…

My Thoughts: Angela Becker

Remember that death is not an end but a beginning. It is hard not to be saddened by thoughts of loved ones passing away. I often think about deaths in the family and wonder what I would do if anything happened to them. It is hard to think of death as a positive natural occurrence. Help me to try to understand that we must all die as Jesus did, and that we only have eternal life to look forward to. Help me be supportive in others' times of trials and needs, and always remember to pray for those souls that have passed away.

My Thoughts: Annette Johnson

There are so many people in the world who possess the framework for a good Christian heart. They've been told the stories and have been shown the way, but so many like me falter in living faithfully in your word and on your path. Help me, Lord, to bring the air of the Spirit into my empty frame.

❧❧•❧❧

Saturday, Sixth Week of Easter

Acts 18:23–28

While Paul was traveling around, he met a person named Apollos. He was a disciple and knew a lot about the Scriptures. He had faith in Jesus, but only up to a point. Paul and his associates, Priscilla and Aquila, filled him in on some of the more up-to-date thinking they had on the belief in Jesus. He was a better preacher about faith in Jesus after that.

Psalm 47:2–3, 8–10 *God is creator and ruler of all the earth*

Clap your hands and shout for joy because God has been so good to us. Sing and sing and sing it with all your heart and soul.

John 16:23–28

Jesus said, "I tell you the truth. Whatever you ask God in my name, you'll receive it. That'll help you a lot when I finally leave."

Further Reflection

Prayer is a powerful part of my relationship with God. I may not always get what I want, but I always get what I need. God's grace is sufficient enough for the day.

Prayer

Dear God, sometimes I think I know exactly what will solve all the problems of the world. Sometimes I even ask you for that kind of power. Please continue giving me what you have always given me, grace enough to get through the day. Please help me to...

My Thoughts: Chris Keyser

God always speaks to us. Sometime we can't hear him, but most of the time, we aren't listening in the right way. God speaks to us through others, through our experiences, and through our happiness and sadness.

My Thoughts: Annette Johnson

Help me not to be ashamed of the joy in my heart. Teach me to live it rather than just believe it.

❧❧•❧❧

SEVENTH WEEK OF EASTER
Monday, Seventh Week of Easter

Acts:19:1–8

While Paul was going around the country, he found some believers who had not received the gift of the Holy Spirit as yet. So after giving them an explanation of what he was talking about, he laid hands on them and conferred to them the power of the Holy Spirit.

Psalm 68:2–7 *Let's sing praises to God for all the good we've received*

Only those who try to live good lives hang around where God abides. The rest stay as far away as they can. So rejoice and sing a song to God, all you who love God. God is a help to all in need.

John 16:29–33

The disciples said to Jesus, "Finally, we understand what you're talking about. We believe that you came directly from God." Jesus answered back, "Do you really believe strongly? A time is coming when you're going to be tested like you've never been tested before! Stick with me to the end and everything will turn out okay."

Further Reflection

Jesus didn't promise his friends that they would have an easy life. He did promise them that they would have eternal life if they believed in him, though.

Prayer

Dear God, I know that some days are up and some days are down. I don't ask you to make them perfect. Just give me enough grace to get through them knowing that you love me always. I can't get through the good days or the bad days without your help, love, and support. Please help me to…

My Thoughts: Elizabeth R. Berning

The bad days are not fun, but they are part of life. Life is not fair or easy. God is always here for me as I travel down the path he has chosen for me. That is what I remember when the days are not so good.

❦❦•❦❦

Tuesday, Seventh Week of Easter

Acts 20:17–27

Paul sent a letter to the people in Ephesus. He told them how he always tried to do God's will and not worry about what people thought or said about him or tried to do to him. He told them his only desire was to do what God wanted of him.

Psalm 68:10–11, 20–21 *Let's sing a joyous song to God*

God, you provide for us all. You are good and wonderful. You help carry our burdens. You saved us from our sins. You are our salvation.

John 17:1–11

Jesus prayed, "God, my time is almost over here. I have tried the best I could to do what you wanted of me. I tried to spread the good news of your love to all I met. I have tried to instill in my disciples your way of life. I know they believe. I entrust them to your care as I return to you."

Further Reflection

Doing the will of God who created us seems to be a recurring theme, not only of Jesus, but of Paul too. When I try to do that in my own life, I seem to be happiest.

Prayer

Dear God, your will, not mine. Your way is what works best. Please help me to…

My Thoughts: AR

So many times I think of what's best for me, or what I need, forgetting what God needs from me and neglecting his plan. So often in prayer I spend more time asking and talking rather than listening. If only I'd give more time for God to answer instead of thinking I know what's best.…I definitely need more patience in opening my heart for his answers.

❦❦•❦❦

Wednesday, Seventh Week of Easter

Acts 20:28–38

Paul said to the elders of Ephesus, "Keep the faith and watch over the people entrusted to you. That's a big responsibility. People will come and try to change the truth that I have taught to you. Don't be sucked in by them. I have to move on to other places, but I left you with all that you need to know about our belief in Jesus. So keep the faith strong." They all prayed together for Paul's safety as he traveled on to new places. There were a lot of tears shed that day because someone they had come to love very much had to move on. Some of them knew they would never see him again in this lifetime.

Psalm 68:29–30, 33–36 *Let's sing a joyous song to God*

God, you provide for us all. You are good and wonderful. You help carry our burdens. You saved us from our sins. You are our salvation. You are awesome and wonderful. All kingdoms should praise you for your greatness.

John 17:11–19

Jesus prayed, "God, please watch over those I will leave behind. I have taught them all about you. They really are no longer of this world. They have set their sights higher. Protect them and help them."

Further Reflection

What a beautiful prayer Jesus made to God on behalf of his disciples. In a sense it is a prayer Jesus made on our behalf, because we are his disciples too.

Prayer

Dear God, help me and protect me and guide me, for without you I flounder and can do nothing. Please help me to…

My Thoughts: Joe Curry

Guide me and lead me when I am weak. Watch over me when I am strong. Help me keep my faith and appreciate and accept the wonderful mysteries of the Catholic Church. Sing a new song unto the Lord for his song is sung from the mountains high.

❧❧•❧❧

Thursday, Seventh Week of Easter

Acts 22:30; 23:6–11

When Paul was brought to court he said on his behalf, "I am a Pharisee from birth. I am of the group who believes in the resurrection." This caused some confusion among those who were judging Paul because some of them believed in the resurrection while some didn't. The dispute got so out of control that they got Paul out of the room for fear that he might have been killed in the thick of it all. That night Paul had a vision that he would go to Rome to preach.

Psalm 16:1–2, 5, 7–11 *God, keep me safe. I put all my trust in you*

God, in you I take refuge. I put you before me at all times. I trust totally in you. You've never let me down. Show me your way and I will follow.

John 17:20–26

Jesus prayed, "I pray not only for my disciples but also for all those to whom they teach the truth. I pray that we all may be one. I living in you. You living in me. We living in them."

Further Reflection

Being at one with everyone is a beautiful thought and a beautiful prayer that Jesus offered to God. It will only happen if I am willing to lay down all the hatred and dissension I harbor in my heart for people who think and look and act differently from me.

Prayer

Dear God, help me to be more willing to be at peace with all the people around me who bug the daylights out of me. Please help me to…

My Thoughts: Nicole Borchardt

Be conscious of all the ways that I break the unity of your body, the Church. As I recognize this resistance to love, help me to bring each person or situation to you for healing. I want to love everyone in theory, but it's hard to get my emotions, actions, and will to carry it out, especially when people don't treat people the way I would like to be treated. Help me to grow closer to this ideal though. So that we really may all be one—God the Father with Jesus with us. A union of all creation with Creator—what a beautiful thought!

❧❧•❧❧

Friday, Seventh Week of Easter

Acts 25:13–21

One of the court officials sent Paul's case to the ruler. He said, "This is a hard case, because we really don't have jurisdiction over the charges that have been placed on Paul. He's a Roman citizen and has the right to be tried in a Roman court. I was wondering what you think about this whole thing?"

Psalm 103:1–2, 11–12, 19–20 *God is ruler over everything*

Let us bless God for all the goodness we have received. God has been so kind and good to all of us. God forgives our sins and everything we have done wrong. God is so good to us.

John 21:15–19

When they were finished eating, Jesus asked Peter, "Peter, do you love me?" "Yes," Peter replied, "You know that already." "Then take care of my people," Jesus said. He asked Peter that two more times. Peter got a little perturbed the third time, and answered Jesus, "You know everything. You know I love you." "Then take care of my people even when things get tough," Jesus replied.

Further Reflection

It's easy to be a follower when everything is going smoothly. It is a little harder when things aren't going the way we'd like them to be going. Jesus warned Peter that this would happen. He encouraged him to stick to it, though. It's almost like Jesus is speaking to us 2,000 years later.

Prayer

Dear God, I need help to practice what I believe. Be near me to encourage me. Please help me…

My Thoughts: Elizabeth R. Berning

I wish I were a better Christian and more vocal about my beliefs. Sometimes I do not stand up for my values and morals. God, help me to be a better Christian and spend more time spreading the good news.

❧•❧

Saturday, Seventh Week of Easter

Acts 28:16–20, 30–31

When Paul finally got to Rome, it took about two years for his case to be heard in court. He was under a type of house arrest, so he did a lot of preaching during the time he was awaiting his day in court.

Psalm 11:4–5, 7 *God, I long to see you face to face*

God is just and full of goodness. God loves those who try to do good. God loves the upright of heart.

John 21:20–25

St. John wrote, "I am a disciple of Jesus and I have written all this down so that you might read it and believe in Jesus, who is our Lord and Savior."

Further Reflection

It's wonderful to see what people of the early Church did and said and thought. It's helpful to see how much this faith in Jesus affected their whole lives. Their faithfulness to the message is encouraging to me to try hard to live my faith because in a sense, it's so much easier than for me to practice my faith. People aren't out there trying to kill me because I believe in Jesus.

Prayer

Dear God, if I complain too much in my prayers, help me to realize how easy I have it today compared to how hard it was to be a practicing Christian in times past. Please help me to...

My Thoughts: Kortney Jendro

The first centuries of the Catholic faith, I think, are the least documented (and considered) by us today. The time when the news of Jesus was new. A fresh air of salvation. Spreading from person to person, town by town. The disciples slowly setting up communities of believers. True missionaries. Perseverance even under threat of arrest, torture, death. What is death to those promised everlasting life?

ASCEND
The Catholic Faith for a New Generation
Eric Stoltz and Vince Tomkovicz

An approachable, clearly written, and contemporary exploration of the Catholic faith aimed at young adults, i.e., the Facebook generation, designed with full-color graphics, short chapters, and interesting sidebar articles that cover the basics of Christianity from a viewpoint that is distinctively Catholic yet ecumenical.

978-0-8091-4621-5

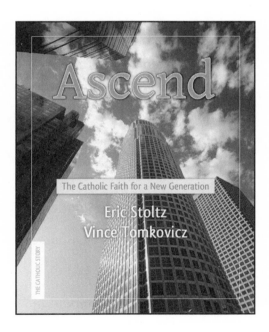

BEING CATHOLIC IN A CHANGING WORLD
Jeffrey LaBelle, SJ, and Daniel Kendall, SJ

"Can I disagree with the Church and still remain a good Catholic?" and "What does it mean to be a Catholic in the post-9/11 world?" These are some of the questions that are posed in this straightforward and accessible book that discusses the key issues surrounding Catholics in today's confusing world.

978-0-8091-4611-6

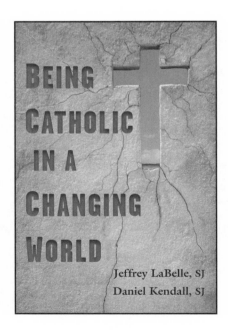

SPIRITUAL MASTERS FOR ALL SEASONS
Michael Ford
HiddenSpring

A blend of the spiritual and journalistic, this book explores the outer characters and inner convictions of the most inspirational figures of recent times.

978-1-58768-055-7

LOSING YOUR RELIGION, FINDING YOUR FAITH
Spirituality for Young Adults
Brett C. Hoover

A guide to helping Gen-Xers reconnect with
spirituality and faith in their lives today. Describes
the lifelong process of discovering both God and self and
explains that for the typical young adult, loss of faith
is a necessary part of maturing spirituality.

0-8091-3782-8

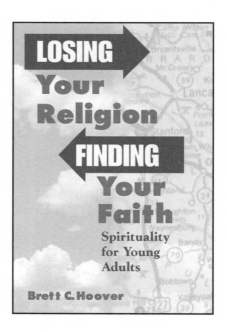

REACTIVATING OUR CATHOLIC FAITH
Reflections to Get Real About Faith
Frank P. DeSiano, CSP

Through eight short, reflective essays, this book
will help people, particularly young adults and parents,
reactivate their Catholic faith by presenting in a
direct way the meaning and purpose behind key
Catholic teachings and practices.

978-0-8091-4597-3

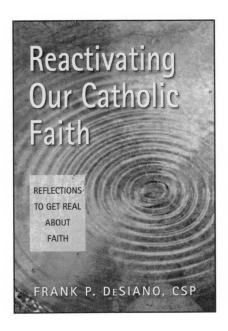

THE DEVIL CAN'T COOK SPAGHETTI
Using Faith to Overcome Fear
Michael Essany
HiddenSpring

Part memoir, part survival guide, *The Devil Can't Cook Spaghetti* is a personal and humorous reflection on coping with the fears inherent to the journey from adolescence to adulthood.

978-1-58768-049-6

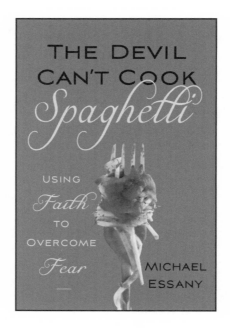

SURVIVAL NOTES FOR GRADUATES
Inspiration for the Ultimate Journey
Robert Stofel
Ambassador Books

These 100 true-life devotionals provide down-to-earth, easy-to-follow suggestions that help graduates as they begin a new and exciting chapter in their lives.

978-1-929039-22-7

STATIONS OF THE CROSS
ACCORDING TO SAINT PAUL
Ronald D. Witherup, SS

A set of images, readings, reflections and prayers in the
context of St. Paul to assist contemporary believers
in reflecting on the passion, death,
and resurrection of Jesus.

978-0-8091-4574-4

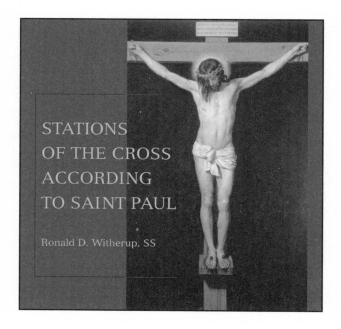

PRAYER OF HEART AND BODY
Meditation and Yoga as Christian Spiritual Practice
Thomas Ryan, CSP; Foreword by Jean Vanier

A practical "how-to" guide for persons who want to
learn how to meditate or practice yoga in a way
that is consistent with their Christian faith.

0-8091-4056-X

A BOOK OF QUIET PRAYER
For All the Seasons, Stages, Moods, and Circumstances of Life
William J. Byron, SJ

This gentle, practical book suggests ways and words
for turning to God in faith, hope, and love, in stages of life,
in all imaginable circumstances. Much more than
a prayer book, it encourages readers to seek
inspiration and compose prayers on their own.

0-8091-4362-3

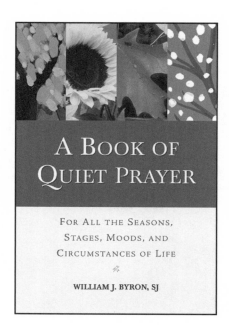